Steam in the
English Landscape

MICHAEL WELCH

Capital Transport

ISBN 978 1 85414 426 3

Published by
Capital Transport Publishing Ltd
www.capitaltransport.com

Printed by Parksons Graphics

Front cover: A photograph taken at Little Bytham on 8th June 1963 during the last few days of rostered through steam working to London prior to the closure of King's Cross shed from 17th June. The photographer was lucky enough to see a real rarity on this section of the East Coast Main Line, Stanier 'Jubilee' Class 6P5F 4-6-0 No.45597 *Barbados*, which worked right through to King's Cross on a special excursion from Bradford Forster Square. *Tommy Tomalin*

Title page: Class 4F 0-6-0 No.44344 wheels a southbound goods working through Kidsgrove station on 27th May 1964. *Tony Sullivan*

Right: Alston station, seen here in this picture taken on 29th March 1964, was originally the terminus of the highly scenic, thirteen miles-long branch from Haltwhistle. It was listed for closure in the Beeching Report and was reprieved, but eventually succumbed on 3rd May 1976 when road improvements in the area had been completed. Nowadays the station is the terminus of a preserved narrow gauge line. *John Boyes/A.R.P.T.*

Back cover: The history of steam traction on the GWR can be traced back as far as 1838 when North Star hauled a Director's special from Paddington to Maidenhead and subsequently the principal locomotive works was established at Swindon. This long tradition of steam traction came to an end, however, in January 1966 when the Western Region triumphantly declared that it was the first BR region to eliminate steam motive power completely, apart from a small number of engines retained for the Somerset & Dorset line. The staff at Oxford shed decided to give steam traction a fitting send off and 'Hall' Class 4-6-0 No.6998 *Burton Agnes Hall* was earmarked for special grooming, the boilersmith apparently making a pair of replica nameplates out of wood which were indistinguishable from the originals. Here, *Burton Agnes Hall* is seen setting off from Oxford in beautiful winter sunshine with the 10.30am Bournemouth to York train on 3rd January; the locomotive worked as far as Banbury and returned light engine. Certainly the end of a glorious era. *Roy Denison*

Introduction

The apple orchards of Kent, the desolate moors of the northern Pennines, the vast expanse of the Somerset levels and the mills and chimneys of industrial Lancashire are all part of England's diverse and much-loved landscape. The railway routes that served England were as varied as the landscape itself and everybody has their personal favourite. Many people love the short but spectacular St Ives branch in Cornwall, some like the coastal stretches of the East Coast Main Line north of Newcastle while others prefer the scenic grandeur of the Middlesbrough to Whitby line.

I have always had a great affection for the heavily-graded Manchester to Leeds route through Standedge tunnel, principally due to past family connections but also as a result of many journeys over the line in steam days. On summer Saturdays in the early 1960s the 9.00am Liverpool (Lime Street) to Newcastle-upon-Tyne was a heavy train, conveyed a restaurant buffet car and was a likely candidate for double heading if resources were available; it certainly would have been banked up the 1 in 59 gradient from Manchester (Exchange) to Miles Platting. This route was very busy with freight traffic and, in addition, there were three engine sheds at the eastern end so railway enthusiasts on the train had to be on their toes. There was a 'Fridays only' steam working, the 5.47pm Manchester Exchange to York, which provided the opportunity for a run over the Pennines behind steam traction until the end of 1967, many years after the principal services had been dieselised.

Apart from the very steep gradients the Somerset & Dorset line (S&D) has little in common with the Standedge line and was essentially a quiet cross-country route serving rural communities, bursting into life on peak summer week-ends when it carried very heavy holiday traffic to Bournemouth and other south coast resorts. The S&D's peculiar status as a joint Midland Railway/

London & South Western Railway venture ensured a bewildering selection of motive power, including the splendid Class 7F 2-8-0s that were unique to the line. Charming unspoilt countryside, beautifully maintained stations and some strange operating practices combined to give this route a unique identity and it had a special place in the affections of many enthusiasts. I was lucky enough to travel over much of the S&D on the footplate, the necessary 'official authorisation' being supplied on the spot by the driver.

My best-loved line by a clear margin is the irresistible and incomparable Settle and Carlisle (S&C) route. Few railway lines rival its absolutely stunning scenery and the breathtaking vistas it offers can only be appreciated from the train which rides high upon the fell side, the roads in the area generally being on a much lower contour. The S&C's infrequent stopping trains were a delight and I can remember a trip in late 1965 on the 4.37pm Carlisle to Bradford (Forster Square) which consisted of three former LMS coaches and a couple of vans hauled by a Stanier 'Black Five'. It was a wet and windy night and when the train stopped at wayside stations lit only by oil lamps there was an eerie atmosphere almost as if civilisation had been left behind. In the summer of 1967 rail aficionados flocked to the S&C to see the last remaining Stanier 'Jubilees' while the very heavy Long Meg to Widnes anhydrite workings provided the ultimate display of raw steam power as they struggled up to Ais Gill summit.

The early railway pioneers were eternal optimists and, perhaps, the line that best illustrated that quality was the Leicester Belgrave Road branch which gave the Great Northern Railway a foothold in the city. The principal trains in pre-grouping days were those to Grantham via Bottesford and Peterborough via Seaton, but even in 1910 services were sparse and the latter were withdrawn as a war time economy measure in 1916 while the Grantham trains were progressively cut back, only two trains surviving by the late 1940s. Regular services lasted until December 1953 while a few local trains specifically for workpeople had to be retained until 1957 due to the reluctance of the local bus company to provide an alternative means of transport. This branch was largely moribund by the late 1950s but excursions for day trippers continued at summer week-ends until September 1962, and it must have been quite a fascinating journey travelling along a line that had such a limited seasonal passenger service but, regrettably, one I never experienced.

The compilation of this book has been quite a challenge at times due to the vast network of routes in England and I have chosen what I hope is a balanced selection of pictures from each of the former BR regions – I soon gave up trying to cover every line due to space constraints. I am very grateful for help received from Bob Dalton, Chris Evans, Dave Fakes and Terry Phillips who have scrutinised my manuscript and suggested many amendments and improvements which, hopefully, have resulted in a much better book. Thanks are also offered to all of the photographers who have kindly supplied digital images or precious original transparencies: without their assistance there would not be a book at all.

Michael Welch
Burgess Hill
West Sussex
January 2018

Contents

The first railway in Cornwall worked by locomotives was the Bodmin & Wadebridge Railway which opened between the towns on 4th July 1834, its main purpose being the haulage of sea sand dredged from the river Camel estuary. On 30th September of the same year the line was extended to Wenford Bridge where the principal traffic was clay, but other minerals including coal and granite were also conveyed; this line never had a regular passenger service. The Wenford Bridge branch, which diverged from the 'main' Bodmin & Wadebridge line at Dunmere Junction, was a delightfully secluded rural backwater which in later years came to prominence because it was worked by three Beattie former LSWR 2-4-0WTs. These diminutive locomotives were the last survivors of an 85-strong class that once worked LSWR suburban trains in the London area and they were retained especially due to the branch's lightly-laid and tightly-curved track. The daily goods train along the branch is seen here crossing the busy A389 main road at Dunmere on 27th August 1962 with Class 0298 No.30587 in charge; this was always a tricky manoeuvre due to the density of road traffic and the crew had to wait for a lull in the constant stream of traffic. *Alan Reeve*

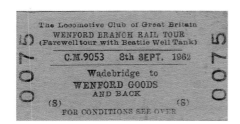

Taken on the same day as the previous photograph, No.30587 stands at Wenford Bridge (known locally as Wenford) prior to returning to Wadebridge with a loaded train. The locomotives based at Wadebridge for use on the branch were Nos. 30585/86/87, three really vintage well tank locomotives built by Beyer Peacock & Co. in the mid-1870s. They monopolised the branch for nearly 70 years but the arrival of former GWR Class 1366 0-6-0PT No.1368 from Weymouth in the spring of 1962 presaged the end of the class's reign on the Wenford Bridge line. This machine underwent clearance trials in the area in May 1962 and ventured up the branch without incident so the writing really was on the wall for the veteran Beattie well tank engines; two further Class 1366 engines arrived from Weymouth. A problem arose, however, with a water tank on the Wenford branch and this needed to be raised before the Class 1366 locomotives could take over. The necessary work was completed in August 1962 and the Beattie locomotives were reportedly taken out of traffic on 8th September and despatched to Eastleigh works where two members were observed later the same month. *Alan Reeve*

The Beattie locomotive waits patiently at Boscarne Junction for a Padstow to Bodmin North train to clear the single line section before it can proceed to Wadebridge. The junction here was the point at which the former GWR line to Bodmin diverged and if the oncoming train seen in this shot had been going to Bodmin General it would have taken the track in the foreground. Compared to the Bodmin & Wadebridge Railway, the GWR was a late arrival on the scene at Bodmin: their branch from Bodmin Road to the General station opened in 1887 with the extension to Boscarne Junction being completed a year later. It is not immediately clear from the photograph but Ivatt 2-6-2T No.41272, which is approaching in the background, carried a small plate on the tanksides indicating that it was the 7,000th locomotive constructed at Crewe Works from where it emerged in September 1950. In contrast No.30587 had already been in traffic for 76 years by that date! *Alan Reeve*

The short two-coach train and emptiness of the surrounding countryside bear testament to the unremunerative nature of the North Cornwall Line. In this photograph an unidentified BR Standard Class 4MT 2-6-4T is beautifully illuminated by the sunshine as it heads westward near Port Isaac Road in August 1964. A few weeks after this shot was taken the pattern of services on the former SR routes in Devon and Cornwall was changed and most operated by diesel traction from that time but the Bude branch and the few Okehampton to Padstow workings remained steam-worked for some time afterwards. DMUs eventually took over but patronage was very poor and on 27th February 1965 the single unit railcar forming the 6.18pm Halwill Junction to Launceston was noted departing with just one passenger aboard, and other trains sometimes ran completely empty. *Alan Reeve*

The North Cornwall Railway, promoted by the LSWR, gained powers in 1882 to construct a line linking Halwill Junction with Launceston and Padstow. The difficult terrain coupled with a shortage of funds meant that progress was slow and the line was opened in stages, the first trains to Wadebridge running on 1st June 1895. A further four years elapsed before Padstow was reached by a line running along the picturesque River Camel estuary, this section opening on

27th March 1899. The line handled a fair amount of goods traffic for many years, principally slate from a huge quarry at Delabole, meat from the farming districts around Launceston and fish from Padstow, the last-mentioned continuing until 1964. This route traversed some of the most attractive countryside in England but it was also very thinly populated and hardly fertile territory for the railway. The summer 1957 timetable advertised only five trains each way along the entire Halwill Junction to Padstow line on weekdays and there was, in addition, a short working to and from Launceston. On Sundays there was a token service as far as Launceston but no trains westward beyond that point. The principal train of the day was undoubtedly the 'Atlantic Coast Express' which left Padstow at 9.35am and arrived in London at 3.40pm, a long journey which was partly explained by the train's slow progress between Padstow and Exeter where numerous stops were made *en route* to serve various small towns. The North Cornwall Line was closed between Halwill Junction and Wadebridge from 3rd October 1966 while the remaining section between Wadebridge and Padstow lost its passenger trains from 30th January 1967. In this portrait the 8.30am Padstow to Exeter Central train is depicted approaching Launceston station on 2nd July 1962 with Bulleid 'Battle of Britain' Pacific No.34084 *253 Squadron* in charge. Patronage could not have been encouraged by the very slow schedules, this train, for example, taking 3½ hours to cover the 88¼ miles. *Tommy Tomalin*

Reflections at Hemyock. The classic view of Hemyock with Class 1400 0-4-2T No.1470 reflected in the placid waters of the river Culm; this picture was taken on 24th June 1961. The milk tankers in the background provide a good clue to the line's staple traffic, this being milk from the Culm Valley Dairy Company's plant at Hemyock which opened in 1886. Consignments of dairy produce kept the Culm Valley branch busy seven days a week and regular milk trains ran to London. The company's factory was across a minor road and milk wagons had to be shunted across with a flagman brandishing a large red 'stop' disc in attendance. Woe betide any adventurous motorists who ignored the flagman's instructions! The line's passenger trains officially ceased from 9th September 1963, with the last services running on 7th September, but few local people apparently took much interest in witnessing the last workings apart from a fair-sized crowd that gathered at Hemyock to witness the final departure. Photographers in the know had one last chance to photograph steam traction on the branch on 23rd August 1964 when the local stationmaster at Tiverton Junction, Fred Pugh, arranged for 1400 Class 0-4-2T No.1450 to haul the regular milk train which had been diesel-worked for some time. Unfortunately, when the locomotive arrived it was in a very scruffy state but the enthusiasts soon got to work putting in some elbow grease to restore it to a respectable condition. The dairy at Hemyock closed in October 1975 thus sealing the fate of this charming rural byway. *John Langford*

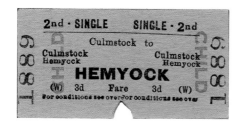

The short length of the train depicted here and the stark fact that in the 1957 summer timetable a paltry service of seven trains departed from Bude station on weekdays vividly illustrate why the branch was tabled for closure in the Beeching Report. The weight of the locomotive and tender probably exceeded that of the train! The branch line from Okehampton (Meldon Junction) to Bude was opened in stages, the first 17¾ miles-long section as far as Holsworthy opening on 20th January 1879. In 1893 a local company obtained an Act to extend the line to Bude but failed to make progress, presumably due to lack of funds, and the LSWR came to the rescue with the result that the first trains over the 10½ miles-long extension ran to Bude on 10th August 1898. Bude station offered the usual facilities, including a refreshment room, while there was a goods shed and turntable and small engine shed where locomotives could be stabled overnight. A particularly noteworthy feature was a short branch to the wharf. While the branch came to life during the summer months, traffic during the rest of the year was insufficient to stave off closure and the inevitable end for the line came on 3rd October 1966. This picture of N Class No.31838 waiting to leave Bude with the 3.09pm to Okehampton was taken on 2nd July 1962. *Tommy Tomalin*

The majority of views taken at Bude feature a train standing at the platform awaiting departure from the station but here, for a change, is a picture taken looking the other way towards Okehampton. The most prominent building is undoubtedly the town's gas works and its tall chimney which dominate the background, overshadowing the railway installations consisting of the water tank, engine shed and signal box. The close juxtaposition of the various buildings tends to create the illusion of an industrial landscape. There was a turntable beyond the shed building and that is where Maunsell 'Mogul' No.31835 appears to be heading prior to hauling a train back to Okehampton. This scene was recorded in August 1964 during the last few months of regular steam traction on the branch. *Alan Reeve*

A Cornish panorama. Despite the overcast conditions the unspoilt Camel estuary still manages to look attractive as N Class 2-6-0 No.31836, hauling the 9.56am Okehampton to Padstow train, crosses the bridge over Little Petherick Creek just outside Padstow; this photograph was taken on 1st August 1963. Padstow was the SR's most westerly outpost and in the 1957 timetable the crack 'Atlantic Coast Express' took exactly six hours to cover the 259¾ miles that separated London's Waterloo terminus and the popular Cornish resort. In the late-1950s Padstow's service comprised no more than five trains on weekdays routed over the North Cornwall Line, but that was very much a rural backwater with limited traffic potential and, therefore, vulnerable to closure in the harsh economic climate that faced the railway industry at that time. The last passenger trains ran between Okehampton and Wadebridge on 1st October 1966 while the line beyond Wadebridge to Padstow succumbed on 30th January 1967. These routes always occupied a special place in the affections of railway enthusiasts and their inevitable closure was mourned by many. *Tim Stephens*

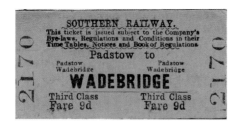

The versatile Maunsell N Class 'Moguls'. In the early 1960s Devon and Cornwall were among the best areas in which to observe these locomotives with no fewer than 30 or so being allocated to Exmouth Junction shed, the locomotives being an everyday sight on the 'Southern' routes in that area. The first 'Mogul' appeared in 1917 and fifteen more were built between 1920 and 1924. In the early 1920s the government was seeking to avoid unemployment at Woolwich Arsenal resulting from the reduction in arms manufacturing and ordered 100 sets of parts for N Class locomotives with the boilers being built by the North British Locomotive Co. in Glasgow. The newly formed Southern Railway eventually purchased parts for 50 locomotives at a very favourable price and they were assembled as Nos.A826 to A875 at Ashford works; other railways also purchased kits of parts. The locomotives proved to be invaluable mixed traffic engines, noted for their rugged reliability, and further examples were constructed by the SR in 1932-34. It should be noted that there were other classes of Maunsell 'Mogul', notably the U Class the first of which entered traffic in 1928; there were also three-cylinder versions of both the N and U classes. The golden sands in the background of this shot provide an immediate clue to its location: yes, it was taken between Padstow and Wadebridge with the river Camel forming a delightful backdrop. This photograph depicts the 12.58pm Padstow to Waterloo service with No.31842 in charge and this scene was recorded on 6th July 1962. *Tommy Tomalin*

A busy Sunday evening at Bere Alston. The 5.25pm Exeter Central to Plymouth train, powered by Maunsell 'Mogul' No.31856, is about to come to a stand at Bere Alston station's southbound platform on 1st July 1962. A train in the opposite direction is also signalled so the station staff would have been well occupied. Barrows of all descriptions litter the platforms while a great deal of green and cream paintwork is on show. Bere Alston was the junction for Callington but that service was cut back to Gunnislake from 7th November 1966, while the main route to Exeter was severed when the Bere Alston to Okehampton section was closed from 6th May 1968. The latter closure was particularly short-sighted and has left Devon and Cornwall solely dependent on the former GWR main line via Newton Abbot which is vulnerable to flooding between Dawlish and Teignmouth. *Tommy Tomalin*

Photographed from the 10.00am SO Mortehoe & Woolacombe to Waterloo train headed by Bulleid Light Pacific No.34068 *Kenley*, the 7.45am Yeovil Town to Ilfracombe with sister engine No.34065 *Hurricane* in charge waits for the road away from King's Nympton on 3rd August 1963. Originally known as South Molton Road, the station served that market town about nine miles to the north-east until the Devon & Somerset Railway opened in 1873; the station's name was changed in March 1951. While passing short local trains here was straightforward, lengthy up trains would have to reverse into a long siding to enable the train travelling in the opposite direction to pass so passing trains here could be a protracted procedure. Note the vintage lower quadrant signal on the right and oil lamps on the platform. There was a goods yard at King's Nympton but this closed from 4th December 1967, while the signal box, which can just be discerned at the far end of the platform, became redundant on 26th July 1970 when the line was singled and the down platform abolished. The line through King's Nympton was opened for business as a broad gauge route by a local concern on 1st August 1854 and was converted to dual gauge from 2nd March 1863 when the LSWR took over. The broad gauge era was short-lived and was finally made redundant from 30th April 1877. *Tim Stephens*

The SR was well-known for a number of named trains, perhaps the most high profile being the 'Brighton Belle' and 'Golden Arrow', both of which were formed of stylish Pullman cars, but the multi-portioned 'Atlantic Coast Express', that connected London with a string of West Country resorts, was undoubtedly the most famous of all. The 'Atlantic Coast Express', or 'ACE' as it was universally known, first ran in 1926 with 'King Arthur' class locomotives as the usual motive power but its operation was suspended for the duration of the Second World War. When it returned in May 1946 the appearance of the 'ACE' had been completely transformed with revolutionary Bulleid Pacific locomotives and handsome Bulleid-designed coaches having replaced engines and carriages from the Maunsell era. By the early 1960s the 'ACE' had the most challenging schedule of any train in Great Britain that was still rostered for regular steam haulage, the 83 miles-long stretch between Waterloo and Salisbury being booked to be covered in 80 min. In this illustration, taken in the early 1960s, the westbound train is seen climbing the 1 in 80 gradient from Seaton Junction to Honiton tunnel with 'Merchant Navy' Class Pacific No.35029 *Ellerman Lines* in command. The last booked eastbound train with steam traction in charge ran on 14th August 1964 following the introduction of a small fleet of 'Warship' class diesel hydraulic locomotives while the final westbound working, on 5th September, was taken by No.35022 *Holland America Line* which ran like an engine possessed to Salisbury, the 83 miles from London being reeled off in a breathtaking 78 min. Some experts pointed out that some of the services newly booked for diesels had been worked by prototype LMS and 'Southern' diesel-electric locomotives in the early 1950s so those trains, strictly speaking, were reverting to diesel haulage! *David Mitchell*

Collett 0-4-2Ts come to the rescue! For years, former LSWR M7 Class 0-4-4Ts were staple motive power on the 4¼ miles-long branch from Seaton Junction to Seaton, a genteel resort on the south Devon coast. The ageing M7s were ousted by DMUs in the early 1960s but in early 1965 the Western Region, which had recently gained large areas of Southern Region territory in boundary changes, was experiencing an acute shortage of DMUs and the unit operating the Seaton branch was commandeered for use elsewhere on the region. Much to the surprise of the railway enthusiast fraternity an emergency timetable was introduced on the branch from 15th February 1965 utilising the last remaining 1400 Class 0-4-2Ts, Nos.1442 and 1450, which were moved from Yeovil shed to Exmouth Junction for duties on the Seaton branch. In this portrait No.1442 is seen standing in the branch platform at Seaton Junction station on 27th February 1965 with the 12.38pm train to Seaton formed of an auto trailer. This type of train had been a hallmark of GWR services for decades so it was really remarkable that the swansong for this traditional GWR method of working was on a 'Southern' branch. *Tim Stephens*

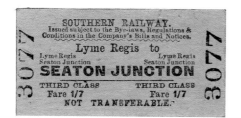

Dulverton was a beautifully maintained, idyllic country junction station where trains on the single track 'main line' from Taunton to Barnstaple connected with those on the Exe Valley line from Exeter and Tiverton. The former was the first line to reach Dulverton, opening throughout on 1st November 1873, while the Exe Valley line, which converged with the 'main line' at Morebath Junction, was brought into use on 1st August 1884. This picture was taken in ideal early morning light at about 7.45am on 16th July 1960 and shows 4300 Class 2-6-0 No.7319 pausing in the eastbound platform with the 6.43am Barnstaple to Taunton train while 4575 Class 2-6-2T No.5573 simmers at the head of an Exe Valley train, probably the 8.10am to Exeter St David's. Note the large station nameboard which advises passengers to change for the Exe Valley line. The service on the Taunton to Barnstaple route on Mondays to Fridays in the summer 1961 timetable comprised six stopping trains each way and these took 1¾ hours on average to cover the 45¾ miles between the two towns. On summer Saturdays pathways had to be found for inter-regional holiday trains with the result that some of the smaller intermediate stations suffered the loss of their service during the middle of the day. There was no Sunday service at any time of the year. The section between Milverton and Norton Fitzwarren was doubled by the GWR in 1937 in order to cater for increasing holiday traffic. The Taunton to Barnstaple route served no large intermediate settlements and some stations were distant from the villages they purported to serve: Dulverton station, for example, was about 2¼ miles from the village so travellers were faced with the choice of a taxi ride or a long walk, the latter not being a prospect to relish on a wet day. The Exe Valley trains were withdrawn from 7th October 1963 while those on the 'main line' lasted almost three years longer. *John Langford*

The four-coach 12.20pm train from Ilfracombe to Taunton awaits departure from Dulverton on 22nd August 1964. The locomotive is 4300 Class 2-6-0 No.5336 which was running without its front number plate. This very successful mixed traffic class was constructed over a long period from 1911 to 1932, the vast majority at Swindon while a small number were built by Robert Stephenson & Co. When this picture was taken No.5336, which dated from December 1917, was in its last weeks of service and was officially withdrawn during September 1964. The last survivors were taken out of traffic later the same year. *Tim Stephens*

Watch out for the fugitives. The station at Melcombe Regis was situated on the branch from Weymouth to Portland and Easton which lost its passenger service from 3rd March 1952 but it was retained until 14th September 1959 for use by summer holiday trains after the branch was closed; goods trains continued until 5th April 1965. Opened as a dual gauge route on 16th October 1865, broad gauge trains down the Easton branch were short-lived ceasing from 18th June 1874. The line had a special signalling system to warn of rock falls similar to that used on the Oban line in Scotland. When rocks cascaded onto the tracks the signals changed their indication to 'danger'. The train seen in this shot taken on 14th August 1960 was a Railway Correspondence & Travel Society rail tour that had originated in London with former SECR L Class 4-4-0 No.31768, an exile from the South Eastern Division of the Southern Region, in charge. Engines were changed at Salisbury with another 4-4-0 taking over, this time T9 Class No.30718 which powered the train down to Weymouth via Yeovil. Former GWR pannier tank locomotive No.3737, a resident of Weymouth shed, worked the train down the branch and is depicted here at Melcombe Regis before setting off down the line. The return journey back to Weymouth was not without incident, the train being halted by police searching for prisoners who had made their escape from Portland prison. After this excitement, which is not normally a feature of RCTS rail tours, the participants returned to London via Fordingbridge. No doubt a very pleasant day out that cannot be enjoyed today. Hopefully the prisoners were soon apprehended. *John Langford*

Unbelievable gradients, stations with lovingly tended floral displays, a confusing mixture of single and double track sections and and some weird operating practices – it is no wonder that the Somerset & Dorset (S&D) was a very popular line among the enthusiast fraternity. The line ran from Bournemouth to Bath and included a branch across the Somerset levels to Highbridge and Burnham-on-Sea. The beautiful countryside and towns along the line were largely unspoilt which added to its undoubted appeal. Even the station names, like Midsomer Norton, Blandford Forum and Shoscombe & Single Hill Halt have a distinct rural charm and it is said that the line was run almost like a family business where everybody seemed to know each other. The northern section of the route from Templecombe to Bath was particularly photogenic due to its fearsome gradients which took the line up to Masbury summit, 811 feet above sea level, in the Mendip hills. Motive power was supplied by Bournemouth and Bath sheds but many people regarded Templecombe, where the S&D connected with the Waterloo to Exeter route, as the nerve centre of the line. The motive power on the route was traditionally of either LMS or 'Southern' origin but in 1958 most of the line was placed under the management of the Western Region (WR) which drafted in a few GWR-designed locomotives to replace some of the traditional stud. This move altered the character of the route and in this shot of Templecombe shed taken on 24th August 1963 Collett Class 2251 0-6-0s and pannier tanks predominate. The stone-built building in the middle of the picture is the old Dorset Central Railway station while the taller brick-built structure is the engine shed which dated from 1950. The single line to Bournemouth is in the foreground while the semaphore signals on the extreme left mark the route of the line into Templecombe station. *Tommy Tomalin*

The location of this photograph is immediately recognisable: yes, it is Evercreech Junction on the much lamented Somerset & Dorset line (S&D). In this picture former Great Western Railway Class 2251 0-6-0 No.3206 is seen leaving with the 1.15pm train to Highbridge on 21st August 1962. When the WR took over control of most of the S&D line locomotives of this type started to appear, especially on the Highbridge branch. The first recorded appearance of a Class 2251 engine, which were totally alien to the S&D, occurred on 31st March 1960 when No.3218 powered a Templecombe to Blandford Forum pick-up goods, this apparently being the first appearance of a former GWR locomotive south of Templecombe since the 1930s. The WR's efforts to introduce former GWR motive power were not always successful, however, and the line's tortuous gradients defied all attempts to employ 5600 Class 0-6-2Ts on the coal trains between Bath and collieries in the Radstock area. On 4th December 1959 No.6641 was noted hauling an empty coal train from Bath to Radstock, later returning with a loaded train, but no further sorties of these engines on the S&D were reported. Presumably the 5600 Class engines were no match for the S&D 2-8-0s which had, after all, been specially designed for the route. *Rail Photoprints*

An event of considerable significance for the S&D occurred on 29th March 1960 when tests were conducted to evaluate the suitability of BR Standard Class 9Fs for use on the line. No.92204 was selected for the trials and, despite appalling weather conditions, took 350 tons over the line unassisted and came through with flying colours. This resulted in the transfer of four members of the class to Bath (Green Park) shed for working the heavy summer Saturday holiday trains, the 9Fs being permitted to take 410 tons unassisted which considerably reduced the amount of double-heading required. Originally, the northern section of the S&D had been constructed as a single line and here the 7.35am Nottingham Midland to Bournemouth West train, headed by BR Standard Class 9F 2-10-0 No.92001, is depicted passing underneath the brick arch of the original bridge which carried the former GWR Witham to Yatton line over the S&D's tracks at Shepton Mallet. When the

line was doubled in 1892 a girder type of bridge was employed proving that the S&D's almost unique ability to fascinate rail aficionados even extended to its bridges. The station was located beyond the bridge and is largely hidden from view, but the roofs of both the station building and signal box can just be discerned. The holiday trains were diverted from the S&D at the end of the 1962 summer timetable and the class 9Fs transferred away. Almost a year later, in August 1963, Bath motive power depot was facing a locomotive shortage and requested the loan of two BR Standard Class 5MTs but was sent two 9Fs instead, Nos.92220 *Evening Star* and 92224. These locomotives were hardly ideal for the line's short local trains, were heavy on coal and were precluded from use on goods working because they were too long for Evercreech Junction's turntable. This picture was taken on 30th June 1962. *Tommy Tomalin*

A helping hand. An unidentified down express headed by BR Standard Class 5MT 4-6-0 No.73051 gets a helping hand from Class 2P 4-4-0 No.40697 over the fierce gradients of the Somerset & Dorset line; the train was photographed approaching Masbury summit on a sunny 7th August 1961. In May 1961 there were seven Class 2P 4-4-0s based on the S&D for use on local passenger trains and piloting the heavier through passenger services, such as the 'Pines Express'. On summer Saturdays the S&D was very busy with through trains from the Midlands and north of England to Bournemouth and many of these required piloting across the Mendips over Masbury summit. The Class 2Ps had their final fling during 1961 because BR Standard Class 4MTs replaced them during the following year. *Martin Smith*

The first passenger train of the day on the up (northbound) line was the 7.00am Templecombe to Bath which is seen here making a brisk getaway from Chilcompton on the rather overcast morning of 24th August 1963, with former LMS 4F Class 0-6-0 No.44167 in charge. Five of these locomotives, Nos.44557 to 44561, were constructed for the Midland Railway specially for use on the S&D line but No.44167 was clearly something of an interloper; it was, however, allocated to Templecombe shed at the time of this photograph. The coaches forming the train comprise three-set No.965 which was one of a batch built by the Birmingham Railway Carriage & Wagon Company for the Southern Railway in the mid-1940s. This set was allocated to the S&D line in November 1959 but was included in the first tranche of withdrawals of Bulleid locomotive-hauled stock which occurred in December 1963. *Tommy Tomalin*

When the WR assumed control of the S&D line it soon became clear that they aimed to eliminate the route as soon as practicable and a manifestation of this policy was the re-routeing of goods workings. Beer traffic from Burton-on-Trent was an early candidate, being re-routed to run via Taunton while, ludicrously, fertilizer trains from Avonmouth to Blandford Forum were diverted to run via Westbury. Those goods trains that did operate carried less and less traffic to which this picture of former S&D Class 7F 2-8-0 No.53806 passing Radstock on 24th August 1963 bears ample testament. The line's motive power in the early days was provided by the Midland Railway (MR), which jointly owned the route with the London & South Western Railway (L&SWR), and it was recognised that the S&D needed locomotives of greater power than the 0-6-0s the MR favoured at the time. The 2-8-0s were designed by Henry Fowler specially for the S&D and constructed in two batches, the first six machines being built at Derby in 1914 while the second series was constructed by Robert Stephenson & Co. at Darlington in 1925. The final survivor, No.53807, was taken out of traffic in October 1964. In the end the 'swift and delightful' S&D was 'sabotaged and defeated' being laid to rest on the evening of 6th March 1966 when one of England's best-loved lines closed for ever. *Tommy Tomalin*

A panoramic view of Castle Cary station, looking westwards, as it was in the 1950s; note the flower beds, milk churns and platform barrows. The main line to Exeter and the west of England diverges to the right while the Weymouth line is on the left. Castle Cary station dates from 1st September 1856 when the Wiltshire Somerset and Weymouth Railway brought into use its broad gauge line from Frome to Yeovil, this being converted to standard gauge in the 1870s. Fifty years elapsed before Castle Cary attained junction status, this occurring in 1906 when the GWR opened its 'new direct route to the west' between there and Taunton, this development making travel between London and the West Country so much easier by substantially cutting journey times. Perhaps the building that stands out most of all is the wartime signal box in the centre of the shot; this replaced the original box which was destroyed by German bombers on 3rd September 1942.
Stuart Ackley collection

Martock station was on the broad gauge branch from Yeovil to Langport West (Curry Rivell Junction) where it joined the main London to Exeter via Castle Cary line; the branch train service ran through to Taunton. The Bristol & Exeter Railway (B&ER) was authorised by an Act of Parliament in 1845 to build a line from Durston Junction, on the Taunton to Bristol line, to Hendford which is just outside Yeovil. It should be noted that the principal route from London to Exeter at that time was via Bristol and many years were to pass before the direct line via Castle Cary was brought into use. Work on the Yeovil branch was a low priority for the B&ER which gave precedence to other projects with the result that the opening of the Yeovil branch was delayed until October 1853. The Wiltshire Somerset & Weymouth Railway line from Frome to Yeovil opened on 1st September 1856 and the line from Taunton (Durston Junction) was extended to connect with the route from Frome. The Taunton to Yeovil line served a predominately rural agricultural area with little prospect of developing new traffic and when passengers were lured away by the growth in private motoring patronage dwindled and the line was proposed for closure which took place from 15th June 1964. This picture of Martock station is thought to date from the 1950s and shows the curious mix of GWR and 'Southern' signalling equipment which was a consequence of the line's takeover by the Southern Region in 1950. It is more than likely that the station nameboard would have been repainted green but it is not quite visible.
Stuart Ackley collection

The first Class M7 0-4-4T emerged from the Nine Elms works of the LSWR in March 1897 and the class eventually totalled 105 locomotives, although it should be noted that some engines had detail differences and were originally classified X14. Many were fitted with pull-push apparatus at various times from 1925. Prior to electrification they could be found on suburban services in the London area and migrated to country districts after their displacement, but a small number continued to be used on empty stock workings to and from Waterloo until the early 1960s. The introduction of diesel units in the late 1950s reduced their sphere of activity and by 1964, apart from one or two miscellaneous duties, they were largely confined to operating pull-push trains on the Swanage and Lymington branches. When this shot of No.30379 hauling the 1.33pm Swanage to Wareham train, which included a through coach to Waterloo, was taken on 15th August 1962 around 35 of these machines nominally survived in traffic but their days were numbered. *Tim Stephens*

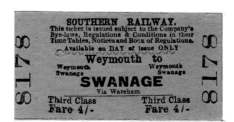

The Didcot, Newbury & Southampton Railway (DNSR) was an independently promoted route authorised in 1873 to construct a railway from Didcot to a junction with the LSWR near Winchester. The LSWR was out of favour in the Southampton area at that time and local entrepreneurs encouraged the DNSR to seek an independent line to the port with a view to developing a through route to the Midlands. In August 1882 the DNSR obtained additional powers for a direct line to Southampton with a terminus near the Royal Pier. The DNSR was faced with dealing with the outright hostility of the LSWR which reluctantly permitted a connection between the two systems just north of Shawford, this being brought into use on 1st October 1891. Initially, the obstructive LSWR did not permit locomotives operated by the DNSR to run on its tracks and engines had to be changed at Winchester. Eventually the DNSR was absorbed by the Great Western Railway. Apart from the relatively large settlements at each end of the route the Newbury to Winchester line served a thinly populated area with little traffic potential but during the Second World War its potential strategic use was recognised. This resulted in an upgrading for military traffic between the Midlands and Southampton, similar to the kind of role that the promoters had envisaged many years previously; the route was closed for seven months in 1942/43, presumably for upgrading work. In this illustration BR Standard Class 4MT No.76017 is depicted at Sutton Scotney with a goods working on 6th February 1960 just a month before the line was closed to passengers on 7th March 1960; goods traffic continued until August 1964. The austere and unashamedly functional wartime signal box would not have won any plaudits for its architectural merits. *John Langford*

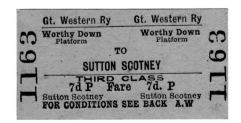

The last train to Hayling Island – 3rd November 1963. Many branch lines have their own individual characteristics but there can be no doubt that the 4½ miles-long Havant to Hayling Island line was in a class of its own. The line was opened by the Hayling Railway on 16th July 1867 which had obtained an Act of Parliament authorising construction in 1860, this long delay being explained by the need to alter the route of the line after it was discovered that serious soil erosion rendered the original choice of route along the western shore of the island impracticable. The line was leased to the LBSCR in 1871 but the local company remained nominally independent. The line was worked in the early years by Sharp Stewart locomotives, the diminutive 'Brighton' Class A1X 0-6-0Ts, universally known as 'Terriers', being introduced on the branch in 1894. There was a severe weight restriction on the wooden trestle Langston bridge which connected the island with the mainland and their weight of 28tons 5cwt made them ideal motive power. In the mid-1920s eleven trains a day were scheduled, a number that had risen considerably by 1948 due to ever increasing holiday traffic during the summer months. In August 1961, for example, a total of 32,000 tickets were collected compared with only 2,000 in March, this emphasising the seasonal nature of operations. During the line's busiest periods a half-hourly service was advertised with a maximum of 24 trains per day. The bridge was vulnerable to ravages of the tide and weather, and had its main timbers replaced in 1903 while, around 1930, the Southern Railway added concrete bases to the timbers. In the early 1960s the condition of the bridge was again causing concern and BR stated that urgent repairs costing £400,000 were required, and expenditure of that nature could not be justified. The line was proposed for closure, the last public passenger trains operating on 2nd November 1963 when a summer Saturday service was run to cater for 'last day' revellers. The following day a Locomotive Club of Great Britain rail tour traversed the branch and is seen here with 91 years-old Class A1X 0-6-0T No.32636 about to pass over the Langston bridge in glorious autumn sunshine, assisted by sister locomotive No.32670 on the rear. *Tommy Tomalin*

The Isle of Wight's railway system became a Mecca for railway aficionados largely due to its vintage rolling stock which BR was unable to replace easily due to the island's physical isolation from the mainland. In the early 1960s rumours circulated that a stud of BR Standard 2-6-2Ts was being sent to the island but in the event the ageing former LSWR O2 Class 0-4-4Ts, most of which had been shipped across by the 'Southern', struggled on to the end of steam in December 1966. Despite the modest traffic potential the island's rail network was quite extensive, stretching from Bembridge, in the east, to Freshwater in the west but cutbacks in the 1950s reduced the system to two principal routes, those from Ryde Pier Head to Cowes and Ventnor. During the 1960s secondary and branch line services on the mainland had benefited from the introduction of more modern Maunsell stock and the Isle of Wight became the only place where it was possible to travel in veteran, pre-grouping wooden-bodied carriages. This resulted in hundreds of enthusiasts making a pilgrimage to the island to experience travel as it was in Victorian days and photograph the delightful O2 Class locomotives which were usually well polished by the staff who took great pride in their everyday job. After a day of intensive operation the locomotives could become slightly grubby which is exemplified here by the condition of No.W33 *Bembridge*, seen here at Ryde Pier Head in glorious evening light on 31st July 1960. *John Langford*

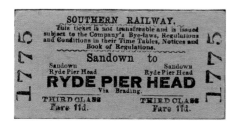
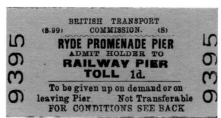

THE VINTAGE SCENE ON THE ISLE OF WIGHT

A total of 73 E1 Class 0-6-0T locomotives was built for the LBSCR to the design of William Stroudley between 1874 and 1884 and six more with slight modifications were constructed during the Billinton era. Four engines were shipped across to the Isle of Wight in 1932/33 and fitted with Drummond-type chimneys and Westinghouse air brakes; they became Nos.1 to 4 in the island's number series and were named. When this shot of No.W4 *Wroxall* was taken at Ryde on 31st July 1960 it was the oldest locomotive on the island, having been built at Brighton Works as long ago as November 1878. Its sister engines had fallen by the wayside, *Wroxall* being the final member of its class left on the island, and it is likely that it was out of use when this picture was taken; it was officially withdrawn in October 1960. *John Langford*

Trains leaving Sandown are immediately faced with a steep incline which has an appealing background of mature trees and this was a favourite location for photographers. Here, No.W31 *Chale* is seen making a steady climb away from the station with a train bound for Ventnor, also on 31st July 1960. Sandown used to be a junction station served by trains to and from Newport but these were a casualty in the mid-1950s, ceasing from 6th February 1956. *John Langford*

The rush hour at Shanklin. The crew of Class O2 No.W29 *Alverstone*, which was powering a train from Ventnor to Ryde, wait impassively for a train in the opposite direction, headed by No.W20 *Shanklin*, to be safely berthed at the southbound platform before they can be on their way to the next stop at Sandown. The station foreman is diligently supervising operations by the foot crossing, one of his most pressing tasks being to ensure that nobody dares to cross the line while there are two trains in the station area. This photograph was taken on 26th June 1964. *Tim Stephens*

Ventnor station was beautifully situated, surrounded by chalk downland on three sides that rose to a height of more than 700 feet above sea level. The station was located at the end of the 1,312 yards-long Ventnor tunnel, a single track bore under St Boniface Down. One of the tracks had platforms on both sides and the facilities included a telephone booth which was no doubt appreciated by holiday-makers who wished to order a taxi to their hotel. An old Southern Railway sign above the station entrance survived until at least 1965 and added to the old-fashioned feel of the place, and the local staff clearly took pride in their station: note the tubs of flowers on the island platform. In this illustration Class O2 0-4-4T No. W27 *Merstone* is seen taking water after arrival with a train from Ryde on 31st July 1960. One can almost hear the rhythmic panting of the engine's Westinghouse brake pump intermingled with the cries of seabirds circling overhead – few stations had quite the atmosphere of Ventnor. The position of the station high above the town could not have encouraged customers, however, and it probably came as no surprise when the Shanklin to Ventnor section of line was closed from 18th April 1966, just before the start of the holiday season. *John Langford*

Towards the end of steam on the 'Southern' the dedication and pride of staff had, perhaps understandably, been undermined by the knowledge that the days of steam traction were numbered. In former times it would have been unthinkable for Nine Elms shed to roster a dirty locomotive to work the 'Bournemouth Belle' but by 1966, the final full year of steam operation, they would probably have been hard pressed to find a clean one! Here, the down train is seen passing Winchfield on 11th June 1966 with filthy Bulleid 'Merchant Navy' Class Pacific No.35012 *United States Lines* in command; at least the locomotive is still carrying its name and numberplates. Class 47 diesels were rostered to haul the 'Belle' from January 1967 but in practice steam substitutions were commonplace and the train was even steam hauled during the very last week of steam working. The history of the 'Bournemouth Belle' can be traced back to 1931 when it ran on Sundays throughout the year and daily during the summer period but it was suspended during the Second World War. After the end of hostilities brand new Bulleid Pacifics were regularly booked to haul it and one can only speculate how people who had suffered the deprivations of the grim war years reacted to the sight of a gleaming 'air smoothed' Bulleid 'Merchant Navy' locomotive leaving Waterloo at the head of a train of immaculate Pullman cars – it must have really lifted their spirits. Note the preparatory work for electrification with newly relaid track and the third rail already in place. The train on the other line is worthy of note as the penultimate coach is one of a fleet of 20 green-liveried, dual heated, vacuum braked Mark II first class corridor vehicles allocated to the Southern Region.
Tommy Tomalin

A scene photographed at Guildford on 3rd January 1965, showing Maunsell N Class 'Mogul' No.31816 about to depart with the 11.50am Reading Southern to Redhill local train; this was the last day of regular steam traction on the route. This is a very appealing cross-country line which follows the escarpment of the North Downs between Guildford and Redhill and in times past long-distance inter-regional trains to the Kent coast used to come this way. Motive power along the line comprised a fascinating selection ranging from graceful LSWR T9 Class 4-4-0s to more modern S15 Class 4-6-0s and BR Standard types. Latterly, the route became famous among the railway enthusiast fraternity as the last stronghold of the Maunsell 'Moguls' which were not finally ousted from passenger workings until 4th January 1965 when diesel units took over. Other scattered workings for those machines continued, however, one of the trains which occasionally produced a 'Mogul' being the 7.30am Woking to Basingstoke. The last four Maunsell 'Moguls' were based at Guildford shed for a variety of mundane duties in connection with the Bournemouth electrification but even these ceased in June 1966 when the remaining locomotives were withdrawn.
Tim Stephens

The county of Surrey survived the Beeching era with almost all of its railway network unscathed, the only notable casualty being the Horsham to Guildford line. The Horsham & Guildford Direct Railway was opened on 2nd October 1865 and the local company had the financial backing of the LBSCR. In the early years the train service consisted of only four trains on weekdays but this level of service was later doubled, with four trains being advertised on Sundays. The LBSCR provided good connections at Horsham for London but those at the Guildford end of the line, where the rival LSWR held sway, were not as convenient and Cranleigh residents in particular regularly voiced their feelings about this situation. The train service was always slow and infrequent well into BR days and, despite a considerable surge in the population of Cranleigh, very little was done to make it more attractive to passengers. So perhaps it was inevitable that when BR proposed closure the government of the day sanctioned this with the usual provision of additional bus services to alleviate any hardship that would be caused. Latterly, this rural backwater was popular with railway aficionados who revelled in the almost undiluted pre-grouping atmosphere and there is no doubt that Baynards station, in particular, was a gem. The station was built to placate Lord Thurlow, who owned land the railway needed to cross, and in return for selling the land at an advantageous price the railway company built a station for his Lordship's use. Latterly, the pride and joy of the staff at Baynards station was a magnificent display of dahlias, some of which are visible in this picture behind the gentleman standing by the signal box, and this riot of colour attracted many visitors. Regrettably, from BR's point of view, very few visitors arrived by train so their only contribution would have been the price of a platform ticket, assuming they bothered to buy one. The train is the 11.35am Guildford to Horsham, formed of pull-push set No.738 plus a ten compartment third vehicle on the rear and the whole ensemble was being propelled by M7 Class 0-4-4T No. 30047; this shot dates from 30th August 1959.
John Langford

2nd - SINGLE	SINGLE - 2nd
Rudgwick to	
Rudgwick Baynards	Rudgwick Baynards
BAYNARDS	
(S) 0/6	Fare 0/6 (S)
For conditions see over	For conditions see over

4675

HORSHAM TO GUILDFORD

Many of the railway routes in Sussex were electrified in the 1930s with steam traction being largely confined to secondary and branch lines, a situation that did not encourage steam photographers. This has resulted in Sussex being one of the least photographed counties in colour in steam days: there was always much more going on in either Kent or Hampshire where main line workings were steam-hauled into the 1960s and, in the case of Hampshire, until steam bowed out on the 'Southern' in 1967. The star turns for steam traction along the West Coast Line from Brighton were three long distance services which connected the south coast town (as it was then) with Bournemouth, Cardiff and Plymouth and in the 1950s they were the preserve of Brighton shed's long-standing quintet of un-rebuilt Bulleid Light Pacifics. When those locomotives were rebuilt they left Brighton and the shed's new allocation of Pacifics was often changed both in terms of the individual locomotives allocated and the quantity: in May 1961 there were six allocated but records reveal that by January 1963 that figure had increased to ten. One wonders why on earth Brighton shed needed so many! In this comparatively rare picture of steam traction at Brighton the 11.00am to Cardiff, with 'West Country' Pacific No.34012 *Launceston* in charge, awaits departure on 15th September 1962. This machine was allocated to Brighton at that time and is in the exemplary condition that was then such a hallmark of the shed. Coincidentally, the task of hauling the very last scheduled steam passenger train from Brighton, a return excursion to Blandford on 11th June 1966, fell to No.34012 but in sad contrast to its condition in this picture *Launceston* was in a deplorable state, encrusted with grime and running without name or numberplates. *Tommy Tomalin*

Enthusiasts throughout southern England mourned the demise of steam on the London to Dover via Tonbridge route which occurred one year ahead of schedule on 12th June 1961. While the big 'switch on' was doubtless hailed by the BR management it is unlikely that they mentioned the cessation of passenger services to Hawkhurst nor the closure to goods of the former Kent & East Sussex line (KESR) both of which coincided with the start of electric services. The Locomotive Club of Great Britain commemorated the virtual end of steam in Kent on Sunday 11th June by organising a rail tour from Victoria which covered both the Hawkhurst branch and the KESR line. Various locomotives were employed during the day including a wonderful combination of Class O1 No.31065 and C No.31592 along the Hawkhurst branch. The run down from Tonbridge to Robertsbridge was entrusted to Class D1 4-4-0 No.31749 piloted by H Class 0-4-4T No.31308 and the pair are seen here in the delightful setting of Robertsbridge station reversing onto the tightly curved KESR line – a tricky manoeuvre indeed. A pair of LBSCR 'Terriers', Nos.32662 and 32670, officiated during the journey to Tenterden during which they became short of breath and had to stop to raise steam. The atmosphere on the train was probably subdued as the participants returned to Charing Cross later in the day but the enthusiasts were safe in the knowledge that they had witnessed historic events that would never be repeated. Apart from steam traction's token presence at Tonbridge, where duties on the Redhill and Tunbridge Wells West lines remained, and Ashford works, Kent had become a 'steam free' county almost overnight. *John Langford*

There were several unsuccessful schemes to construct a railway line to serve the High Weald of Kent before the South Eastern Railway eventually opened a branch from Paddock Wood, on the main Charing Cross to Dover route, to Hope Mill (later Goudhurst) in 1892. In September 1893 an extension to Hawkhurst was brought into use and in addition to Goudhurst there were intermediate stations at Horsmonden and Cranbrook. The route crossed a series of parallel ridges so it was something of a switchback line with constant changes of gradient: some of the inclines were quite severe such as the 1 in 60 which faced southbound trains between Goudhurst and Cranbrook. The modest Horsmonden station is depicted in this portrait taken on 10th September 1960 and an oast house, so typical of this part of Kent, towers above the rather squat station building which appears to have been the beneficiary of a fresh coat of paint. It certainly looks spick and span - didn't anybody tell the painting team that the line had been proposed for closure? It was a sad day when the last regular passenger train ran on 10th June 1961 and this charming line has since faded into history. *John Langford*

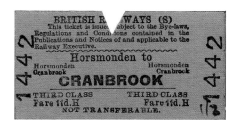

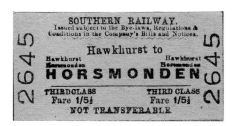

The cream-and-green painted buildings, so redolent of the 'Southern', stand out in this picture of Cranbrook station which was taken during the branch's last full month of service on 6th May 1961. A train bound for Hawkhurst with H Class 0-4-4T No.31500 in charge simmers in the platform; note its duty number displayed on the headcode disc. Like other stations on the line, Cranbrook station's facilities were basic in the extreme, consisting of a simple single-storey corrugated iron building with a small wooden awning. The stationmaster's substantially-built three-storey house was almost palatial in comparison, the only possible drawback being its remoteness from the village. Note the train is made up of Maunsell carriages converted for pull-push operation rather than a pre-grouping set. *Roy Denison*

The Southern Region had a nasty habit of combining the train service along various routes into one table and in 1957 summer timetable the Paddock Wood to Hawkhurst branch, rather than have its own separate table, was hidden away in the all-encompassing, 51-page, table No.20 which covered London to Hastings, Folkestone and Margate! This reveals that the branch's timetable on Mondays to Fridays consisted of six return trains and, inevitably with such a meagre service, there were long gaps during the middle of the day; the 11½ miles-long journey took on average half-an-hour. The Hawkhurst branch is probably best known for the hop-pickers' specials which brought trainloads of Londoners down from the smoky capital but these declined throughout the 1950s. In this portrait former SECR C Class 0-6-0 No.31588 stands at the buffer stops of Hawkhurst station after arrival with the 9.40am 'hop-pickers' friends' special from Paddock Wood on 11th September 1960. Presumably by this date the traditional through workings from London had ceased to run and a connection at Paddock Wood was the best that could be hoped for; in this case the train seen here had connected with the 8.28am London Bridge to Maidstone West, hauled by Class E1 No.31067. The ambitious promoters of the line originally planned an extension with Rye as their goal, hence Hawkhurst was built as a through station, but their dreams were never turned into reality. *John Langford*

Farewell to the 'Westerham Flyer'. The history of the Westerham branch can be traced back to 1860 when the South Eastern Railway (SER) obtained powers to build a branch from Dunton Green, on the main London to Tonbridge line. Those powers lapsed and local landowners and traders, who were anxious to connect their town with the expanding railway network, secured the incorporation of the Westerham Valley Railway Company. Later the SER agreed to manage, maintain and operate the line which eventually opened on 7th July 1881 with one intermediate station at Brasted; Chevening Halt was added in 1906. The 4¾ miles-long line was originally built as a double track formation but only one track was laid. Unfortunately, the town of Westerham is quite close to Oxted and many local commuters considered it was more convenient to drive to Oxted and take the train from there in preference to using the branch service and changing at Dunton Green. The last day of passenger services was 28th October 1961 and here former SECR H Class 0-4-4T No.31518, emblazoned with chalked inscriptions and a Union Flag, is seen propelling the 1.05pm from Westerham into Dunton Green station on that date. Presumably, the Union flag was one of the de luxe fire-resistant variety!
Tim Stephens

Another shot taken on the last day of the Westerham branch showing Class D1 4-4-0 No.31739 taking the 2.50pm Dunton Green to Westerham between Chevening Halt and Brasted. The traditional two-coach pull-push set formed the 2.23pm ex-Westerham and then left the stage, its place being taken by the Class D1 and seven coaches that had come down from London. No.31739 was assisted by Class Q1 No.33029 from Tonbridge shed and the two locomotives worked alternate trips, this being due to the limited run-round facilities at Dunton Green. The final train was the 8.30pm from Westerham worked by the Q1 and when that departed the curtain came down on this relatively unknown branch line. *Tim Stephens*

The Great Western Railway (GWR) was incorporated on 31st August 1835 to construct the line from London to Bristol and briefly flirted with the idea of sharing Euston station with the London & Birmingham Railway, but this was rendered impracticable by the GWR's choice of the 7ft gauge. A site near Paddington village was decided upon and services to Maidenhead started on 4th June 1838 while those to Bristol commenced on 30th June 1841. The premises were progressively enlarged and modernised over the years, notable landmarks being the addition of four platforms under a new roof span in 1909 and the lengthening of platforms plus the installation of colour light signalling in 1933. Paddington station's glory is its magnificent triple-arched roof, once described as a 'unique work of art remarkable for its many qualities'. Many steam enthusiasts would opine that the 'King' Class 4-6-0s were in very much the same category, unique works of art in their own right. In this illustration a member of that illustrious family, No.6015 *King Richard III*, stands at Paddington awaiting departure with a Wolverhampton express on 23rd June 1962. The last months of 1962 saw the withdrawal of all the 'King' Class locomotives which were for some years the most powerful steam locomotives in Great Britain. Constructed to Collett's design, a total of 30 locomotives was built between 1927 and 1930 but due to their weight they were restricted initially to the London to Plymouth and London to Wolverhampton via Bicester routes where they hauled the heaviest expresses. Their rapid withdrawal was due to the mass invasion of diesel hydraulic locomotives onto the WR which displaced them almost overnight from their traditional stamping grounds. Despite its official withdrawal, No.6018 *King Henry VI* was steamed especially for a Stephenson Locomotive Society 'Farewell' special train in April 1963, all its sister engines having been withdrawn by the end of 1962. *Rail Photoprints*

The dead straight main line tracks, the tall water softening plant with its adjacent water tank and the engine shed in the distance: the view from the long footbridge at Southall is unmistakable and in this portrait Class 8750 0-6-0PT No.9641, pulling a substantial goods train from Brentford, adds considerable interest to the scene. A diesel unit approaching Southall station from Paddington can also be seen in this shot which was taken on 25th September 1962. The branch from Southall to Brentford has an eventful history, being closed to passenger traffic during the First World War from 22nd March 1915 and reopened some time after the end of hostilities on 12th April 1920. History repeated itself to a degree during World War Two when the branch was closed again, presumably as an economy measure, from 4th May 1942 but on this occasion it never reopened to passenger trains. *Martin Smith*

'Services in the Southall area may be subject to delay owing to a temporary obstruction on the line'. In this portrait Class WD 2-8-0 No.90261 slowly makes its way from the down slow line to the west sidings with a very long train of empty wagons; this shot was taken on 11th September 1961. A grand total of 934 of these unglamorous 'Austerity' 2-8-0s was built by the North British Locomotive Co. and Vulcan Foundry during the Second World War for the Ministry of Supply, some of which were sent overseas never to return; many saw service in France, Holland and Belgium. The engine depicted here was built by the North British Locomotive Co., outshopped in September 1943 as WD No.77368 and was one of 422 (later Nos.90000 to 90421) locomotives of the class built by that company and subsequently entered BR stock. Another sizeable batch (later Nos.90422 to 90732) was constructed by Vulcan Foundry and altogether 733 entered BR service. During BR days these engines were particularly associated with the haulage of heavy mineral trains in northern England but they were based on all BR regions at some stage, including the 'Southern' for a time in the early 1950s. Many locomotives that went overseas during the Second World War never returned to Great Britain but one example, WD No.79257, went to Holland and was sold to the Swedish State Railways in 1952. It was repatriated in 1973 and at the time of writing can be seen on the Keighley and Worth Valley Railway. *Martin Smith*

An evening scene photographed at Euston station on 12th February 1964 with 'Princess Coronation' Pacific No.46250 *City of Lichfield* simmering at the buffer stops after arrival with the 10.53am from Workington (Main). A Sulzer Type 2 diesel makes an unwelcome intrusion on the left of the picture. In the summer 1963 timetable this train had an advertised arrival time in London of 7.22pm (7.40pm on Fridays) and its schedule was probably vastly inflated to allow for engineering works which were at their height on the West Coast Main Line at that time. Between Workington and Carnforth this train stopped at most stations and was virtually a local service, but at least it provided the convenience of through carriages to the capital. After such a marathon journey passengers from Workington were doubtless relieved when they eventually arrived in Euston. *Tim Stephens*

Pacific power unleashed. The date was the 17th July 1962 and judging by the sparkling light at South Kenton a really lovely summer day appeared to be on the cards as 'Princess Coronation' Class Pacific No.46235 *City of Birmingham* hove into view at the head of an early morning departure from Euston. The Pacific was already bowling along apparently unrestrained by its huge load of about 14 vehicles forming the 6.35am Euston to Windermere and Whitehaven Bransty: note the vans marshalled behind the third coach indicating that the train would be split *en route*. The engineers were in constant occupation of the West Coast Main Line at this time and services from Euston were drastically curtailed, the 6.35am being scheduled to run via Northampton and stop at virtually every station of any consequence, this being reflected in its arrival time at Crewe of 11.24am. The advertised arrival time at Whitehaven Bransty was 4.49pm with that portion being routed via Keswick and Workington. It may have been slow but what a journey! *Martin Smith*

The London & North Western Railway's (LNWR) G2A Class 0-8-0s were without doubt one of the most distinctive designs to survive into the 1960s in any great number. A total of 572 (including the G2 class) was constructed of which 502 were inherited by BR and, interestingly, the first member of the G2A class was condemned as long ago as 1921 due to a boiler explosion. The history of this class, known to railwaymen as 'Super Ds', is extremely complicated with various LNWR Chief Mechanical Engineers being responsible for rebuilding engines at various times as compounds and 2-8-0s(!) in addition to fitting different types of boilers. The locomotive seen here is No.49377 which was working a heavy goods train at Stonebridge Park on 13th April 1962; note that it is fitted with a tender cab, a blessing when working tender-first on a cold day but a curse on a hot summer day. This engine was built at Crewe and was one of 170 four-cylinder compound locomotives that entered service between 1901 and 1904; this particular example entered traffic in November 1902. Later in its career No.49377 was fitted with a higher pressure boiler and was reclassified from G1 to G2A. It was quite a widely travelled locomotive during its life, being allocated to Sutton Oak shed in the early 1950s and then, perhaps surprisingly, Warwick in 1958. The vast bulk of Stonebridge Park power station, with its two massive chimneys reaching skywards and adjacent cooling tower, dominate the background and the entire scene is more reminiscent of the grimy, industrial north of England rather than a location in north-west London a little over a mile from Wembley stadium. *Martin Smith*

Looking for all the world a true thoroughbred, former GWR 'King' Class 4-6-0 No.6029 *King Edward VIII* is getting into its stride at North Acton with the 12.10pm Paddington to Birkenhead (Woodside) express on 24th May 1962. The van formed immediately behind the locomotive was known to railwaymen as a 'Fruit D', a classic GWR design. The West Coast Main Line was in the throes of electrification at this time and an enhanced service was operating from Paddington to Birmingham and Wolverhampton with steam traction very much to the fore. Crew training on replacement 'Western' Class diesel hydraulic locomotives had already begun in the West Midlands, however, and full diesel working was introduced from 10th September 1962. No.6029 had already been withdrawn by that date and when the 'Westerns' took over no fewer than thirteen 'Kings' were immediately taken out of traffic, and the class had disappeared completely from everyday service by the end of the year. Would the WR ever be the same again? *Martin Smith*

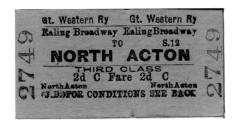

Photographed in ideal evening lighting conditions, BR Standard Class 9F 2-10-0 No.92183 emerges from Hadley North tunnel with a down goods in June 1963. The section of line between New Barnet and Potters Bar had been an operational bottleneck where three tunnels in 2½ miles made improvement difficult and, no doubt, extremely expensive. In the mid-1950s BR embarked on a widening scheme to quadruple that section, thus considerably alleviating the problem. The widening was completed on 3rd May 1959 but by the time this picture was taken the entrance to the new tunnel had already been blackened by smoke. *Martin Smith*

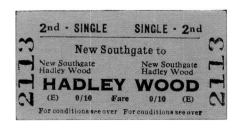

The London & Blackwall and Eastern Counties railways joined forces to promote a line from Forest Gate Junction to Southend via Tilbury and this was opened throughout on 1st March 1856. Trains carried Bishopsgate and Fenchurch Street portions which joined and divided at Stratford, but this procedure was time consuming and on 7th July 1856 a cut-off was authorised between Barking and Gas Factory Junction (Bow) with running powers straight into Fenchurch Street. An extension to Shoeburyness was opened in 1884. During this period the resort of Southend saw phenomenal growth and in order to cater for the burgeoning business traffic a cut-off from Barking to Pitsea via Laindon was sanctioned in 1882 and opened throughout on 1st June 1888. The system had been leased to the contractors Peto, Brassey and Betts since 1854 but in 1875 the lease expired and the London, Tilbury and Southend Railway (LTSR) took full control. In more recent years many trains were worked by a fleet of 37 Stanier Class 4MT 2-6-4Ts which were built at Derby in 1934. These machines were constructed specifically for the LTSR and had three cylinders and other detail differences compared to Stanier's other 2-6-4T classes; they were allocated to Shoeburyness shed at this time. Here, No.42514 is depicted racing along between Upminster and West Horndon with the 10.10am Fenchurch Street to Shoeburyness train on 31st October 1961. *Tim Stephens*

The Stanier 2-6-4Ts did not have the monopoly on the LTSR line, however, and in 1961, the year immediately before the route was electrified, Tilbury shed had an allocation of 22 BR Standard Class 4MT 2-6-4Ts while Shoeburyness also boasted a small allocation of Fairburn 2-6-4Ts. One of these machines, No.42227, is also seen between Upminster and West Horndon, this time working the 3.25pm Fenchurch Street to Shoeburyness train on 1st October 1961. This locomotive was a really modern machine, being out-shopped from Derby Works in May 1946 towards the end of the LMS era. When it was withdrawn in October 1962 it probably had many years of service life remaining. *Tim Stephens*

The first terminus of the Great Eastern Railway (GER) in London was at Shoreditch but this was cramped and inconveniently sited for the City so in 1865 the GER obtained an Act to build a very costly extension to Liverpool Street which opened in 1874/75. This terminus was later known as the West Side after further development took place in the early 1890s which resulted in the opening of the East Side of the station. The latter caused the destruction of workers' dwellings and the Parliamentary Act stipulated that the GER was obliged to provide cheap tickets to enable the relocated workers to reach their workplace in the metropolis. The original Shoreditch terminus was retained as a goods depot but was gutted by fire in 1964. One of the benefits of the piecemeal development of Liverpool Street was the location of a strategically situated taxicab road which separated the two halves of the station and provided an ideal grandstand for train spotters.

Some spotters can just be seen in this shot of BR Standard 'Britannia' Pacific No.70007 *Coeur-de-Lion* standing over a pitted road where basic servicing was carried out on locomotives between duties. No.70007, which is in the customary clean condition for express passenger engines on the GER main line, appears to be raising steam while the fireman is emptying the ashpan. Note the water crane and brazier, two absolutely essential infrastructure items in the steam age. A shiny new diesel can be seen lurking menacingly in the background together with an L1 Class 2-6-4T. *RCTS Archive*

Introduced in 1914, the Class N7 0-6-2Ts were primarily designed to replace a motley collection of classes used on the busy suburban services out of Liverpool Street and at the grouping twelve locomotives were already in service with another ten under construction at Stratford Works. Gresley continued to develop the design and a total of 134 was eventually built by a variety of builders including outside contractors. No.69621, which entered traffic in March 1924, was the last locomotive to be constructed at Stratford works. The class will always be identified with the suburban trains to and from Liverpool Street, and in times gone by the service was known as 'Jazz Trains' due to the class of travel being denoted by a colour code at door-top level. In 1919 track rearrangements and signalling improvements were undertaken at Liverpool Street with the aim of reducing conflicting movements and short engine sidings were laid to ease congestion. This was the ultimate step in managing a dense, steam operated suburban service, one of the most intensive in the world. Some of the Class N7 engines used on the suburban service were maintained in exemplary condition by Stratford and other sheds and the crews were apparently paid a little extra for keeping the Liverpool Street pilot in particularly smart condition. Unfortunately No.69668, seen here passing Bethnal Green on an empty stock working from Thornton Fields sidings, was certainly not in sparkling condition but this picture was taken on 23rd June 1961 by which time the days of steam were numbered and standards were slipping. *Colour-Rail*

A Liverpool Street to Clacton express with Class B17 No.61630 *Tottenham Hotspur* at its head awaits departure from Thorpe-le-Soken some time in June 1956. A total of 73 of these machines was built between 1928 and 1937 during the Gresley era primarily to replace the Class B12 4-6-0s on the GER main line and later locomotives were built for other routes, particularly the Great Central line. The class was known as the 'Sandringhams', the name originating from the first member of the class to enter service in late 1928. The first 48 engines were named after country houses with most of the remainder being named after football teams. Thorpe-le-Soken is a junction station where the line split with the branch going to Walton-on-the-Naze and the 'main line' to Clacton-on-Sea. It was originally opened by the Tendring Hundred Railway on 28th July 1866 and known at that time as 'Thorpe'. The station was renamed Thorpe-le-Soken on 1st March 1900. *Colour-Rail*

A neglected Class J15 0-6-0, No.65477, hauling two coaches, rolls into Lavenham station on a sunny August day in 1959. The Long Melford to Bury St Edmunds line, opened on 9th August 1865, was probably as pretty a rural route as one would wish to see but with only three small intermediate stations traffic prospects were not exactly rosy. When the line closed to passengers on 10th April 1961 the passenger service was down to a mere four trains each way a day: goods services clung on until April 1965. The signal box seems to have been in use at the time this shot was taken and there are two regulation fire buckets visible; note the traditional gas lighting, 'sausage' station signs and cattle dock behind the box. *Colour-Rail*

A train from Norwich (Thorpe) to Liverpool Street with Class B1 No.61223 in charge runs into Stowmarket station on 20th June 1959; note the mixed rake of maroon plus crimson and cream rolling stock. The signal box with its adjacent starting signal and water crane add interest to the picture. The signalman's job at Stowmarket was probably quite stressful at times because he controlled the level crossing gates across a main road and stopping the flow of traffic must have been quite a task on occasions. *Colour-Rail*

The Colchester Stour Valley Sudbury & Halstead Railway opened the Marks Tey to Sudbury line on 2nd July 1849 while the extension on to Shelford was opened throughout by the Great Eastern Railway on 9th August 1865. When competition from road transport really started to hit their receipts BR sought to close the entire Marks Tey to Shelford line but permission to abandon the first section as far as Sudbury was refused; the remainder was not so fortunate, however, and trains were withdrawn from 6th March 1967. Here, Class D16/3 No.62574 is depicted at Sudbury, presumably heading along the Stour Valley line towards Haverhill and Cambridge. This locomotive first saw the light of day at Stratford works in November 1909 but was rebuilt during its career, losing its decorative valancing in the process. This photograph was taken in February 1954 which proved to be the machine's last full year in traffic as it was withdrawn from service in December 1955. The last survivors of this famous class survived until late 1960. Note the horse boxes in the dock siding and very tall concrete post signal. *Colour-Rail*

The early withdrawal of steam traction from East Anglia meant that relatively few pictures were taken in colour and, perhaps, the largely flat landscape did little to encourage enthusiasts. Judging by the number of pictures submitted for this album the Stour Valley Line seems to have been an exception and in this charming shot another Class D16/3 4-4-0 is seen at Stoke station on 24th September 1956. The locomotive depicted is No.62510 which at the time of the photograph was one of the oldest survivors of this celebrated 'Claud Hamilton' class, having been built at Stratford works in July 1900, although it should be borne in mind that it underwent extensive rebuilding in the 1930s. No.62510 was in its final year of service and was withdrawn from traffic in September 1957. Note the vintage Great Eastern Railway carriage marshalled immediately behind the locomotive. The station actually served Stoke-by-Clare, one of a number of pretty villages that nestle in the Stour Valley. *Rail Photoprints*

Another shot on the attractive Stour Valley Line, this time showing former Great Eastern Railway Class J15 0-6-0 No.65445 pausing at Haverhill in August 1958 with a train consisting of three coaches and a Southern Railway-designed parcels van. No.65445 was one of 289 examples built between 1883 and 1913, this particular engine dating from August 1899; it survived until August 1962. The very light axle loading of these engines made them ideal for working some of the lightly-laid East Anglian branches, such as the Snape branch. The Cambridge University Railway Club used to run an 'Engine Driving and Firing Special' each spring between Linton and Haverhill on the Stour Valley Line and in 1958 the engine employed was the last surviving Class E4 2-4-0 No.62785 which had been beautifully turned out by Cambridge shed. The 1960 summer timetable advertised six stopping trains in each direction along the line on weekdays while on Sundays trains ran this way from Cambridge to Clacton-on-Sea for day trippers but these only called at one or two intermediate stations. *Colour-Rail*

A shaft of sunlight breaks through the otherwise overcast sky at Marlow station on 8th April 1962 brightening the scene as Collett Class 1400 0-4-2T No.1445 simmers between duties; a cloth-capped gentleman is busy washing down its coach with a hosepipe, brush and bucket of water. The line from Maidenhead to Marlow Road (later Bourne End) was opened by a local company on 1st August 1854 and the close proximity of the latter station prompted a group of businessmen in Great Marlow to propose a link to connect with the 'main line'. The result was the Great Marlow Railway Act which was authorised on 13th July 1868 with a share capital of £18,000, one third of this amount being raised locally while the balance was provided by the GWR. The 2¾ miles-long branch from Marlow Road to Marlow was opened on 27th June 1873 and the name of the former station was altered to Bourne End to avoid confusion among travellers. Known affectionately as the 'Marlow Donkey', the summer 1961 timetable lists around ten weekday shuttle trains between Marlow and Bourne End supplemented by through trains from Paddington formed of diesel units. Regrettably, the steam hauled 'Donkey' ran for the final time on 8th July 1962 when DMUs took over the complete service. *Martin Smith*

2nd · SINGLE	SINGLE · 2nd
Bourne End to	
BourneEnd	BourneEnd
Marlow	Marlow
MARLOW	
(W) 9d	Fare 9d (W)
For conditions see over	For conditions see over

9042 9042

The Great Western Railway was noted for the immaculate appearance of its main line steam locomotives which was heightened by their shining copper-capped chimneys and gleaming safety valve bonnets, and this tradition continued well into BR days. Swindon works was the principal centre for heavy overhauls of the steam fleet where the quality of the workmanship and attention to detail was probably unsurpassed anywhere in Great Britain. When this picture of No.4092 *Dunraven Castle* was taken at Swindon on 28th June 1959 diesels had started to arrive but the works was still busy with steam overhauls as exemplified here by this shot. This locomotive was built at Swindon, entered service in August 1925 and survived until December 1961, so it is reasonable to assume this was its last overhaul. *John Langford*

Were all fans of Great Western locomotives obliged to pay homage at Swindon at least once in their lives? If not, perhaps a visit should have been obligatory. In this portrait two gleaming express passenger locomotives and a more humble pannier tank locomotive bathe in the sunshine at Swindon shed on 16th June 1957. The engines are (from l. to r.): 'County' Class 4-6-0 No.1004 *County of Somerset*, 'Castle' Class 4-6-0 No.5062 *Earl of Shaftesbury* and the somewhat less impressive tank engine is 8750 Class 0-6-0PT No. 4612. The last mentioned may not have been the largest of the three engines on display but at least it was a member of the largest class numerically on BR. The 'Counties' were a Hawksworth design, the first example appearing from Swindon works in August 1945, and a total of 30 machines was constructed with the last being out-shopped in the spring of 1947. These locomotives were distinct from all other Great Western designs in that they had one long splasher covering all of the driving wheels and straight, rather than curved, nameplates. *Rail Photoprints*

A party of enthusiasts who visited Swindon works on 17th June 1962 recorded a wide variety of steam power receiving overhauls though it is not known how many locomotives were being given general overhauls bearing in mind the WR was being flooded with diesels at that time. There were many 'Hall' Class engines in for repair plus five BR Standard Class 9F 2-10-0s and four 'Castles', including No.7029 *Clun Castle*. Perhaps the most amazing sight was that of 9700 Class 0-6-0PT No.9703 still lettered 'GWR'! One of the engines 'on works' on that date was Class 5205 2-8-0T No.5206 which was photographed on 12th August enjoying the unaccustomed hospitality of Swindon shed's roundhouse before it returned to its home shed of Aberbeeg in south Wales. In the background is 'Castle' Class 4-6-0 No.7034 *Ince Castle* which was a Gloucester-based locomotive and probably one of Swindon shed's regular guests. *Rail Photoprints*

Anyone for Marlborough? A peaceful scene at Savernake (Low Level) on 26th August 1961 with 8750 Class 0-6-0PT No.3763 waiting in the up bay platform with the 5.33pm train to Marlborough. This service was presumably intended to connect with the 4.36pm from Newbury which was due at Savernake at 5.10pm. An irregular service of slow and semi-fast main line trains served Savernake (Low Level) and the timetable to Marlborough was supposedly designed to fit in with those as much as practicable. The Marlborough service has an interesting history, having been diverted as long ago as March 1933 to run to Savernake (High Level) station, but this was closed from 15th September 1958 resulting in the service reverting to the Low Level station. The summer 1961 timetable lists a paltry five local trains each way between Savernake and Marlborough on Mondays to Fridays with a couple of extras on Saturdays; two trains operated in each direction on Sundays. The service was withdrawn at the end of the summer 1961 timetable. *John Langford*

The train service between Cheltenham and Andover along the former Midland & South Western Junction Railway was extremely sparse and earmarked for closure, as previously mentioned, at the end of the summer 1961 timetable. In this picture, taken at Marlborough on Sunday 27th August 1961, nicely cleaned Class 4300 2-6-0 No.6327 awaits departure with the 9.35am Swindon to Andover Junction train which was booked to call at 10.16am. The summer 1961 public timetable reveals that the weekday service consisted of three trains between Swindon and Andover but, rather strangely, only two in the reverse direction, although there were one or two unbalanced short workings to add to passengers' confusion. The 1.52pm from Cheltenham (St James) to Southampton Terminus (arr. 5.37pm) was obviously the crack train of the day but remarkably no corresponding service was advertised in the reverse direction. On Sundays prospective travellers were obliged to choose between the 9.35am and 5.45pm departures from Swindon and return workings from Andover at 12.40pm and 8.35pm. A trip on this little-known rural byway with its eccentric and irregular passenger service must have been a delight for railway aficionados but, regrettably, the line was closed just a few weeks after this scene was recorded and only the few lucky ones ever experienced its attractions. *John Langford*

The Class 9F 2-10-0s were undoubtedly one of the most successful BR Standard designs, their prodigious haulage capacity on heavy goods trains being complemented by their ability to work passenger trains when the need arose, so they were very versatile machines. Perhaps their finest passenger work was accomplished on the fearsome gradients of the Somerset & Dorset line where their use obviated the need for double-heading on the heavy holiday expresses. The Class 9Fs were particularly associated with the haulage of mineral trains to the London area along the former Midland and Great Central lines, but they were based at sheds in many parts of Great Britain with the exception of Scotland which instead had an allocation of former War Department 2-10-0s. Many of these Class 9F locomotives fell victim to the rapid dieselisation of the BR network and some were broken-up after only five years in traffic. This view depicts No.92152 passing Berkeley Road station, between Bristol and Gloucester, on 18th June 1961 hauling just the kind of traffic for which it was designed. Built at Crewe, this engine entered service in October 1957 and was withdrawn after a mere ten years' service in November 1967. Perhaps best known as the junction for Lydney, in the summer 1961 timetable Berkeley Road station had an unattractive service of around six stopping trains in each direction on Mondays to Fridays, mostly between Bristol and Gloucester. The 6.15pm departure, however, went through to Birmingham New Street where its booked arrival time was 9.32pm so this working was clearly not intended for passengers in a hurry. *John Langford*

Gloucester shed was home to most of the last remaining Class 1400 locomotives which were employed on the Chalford and Sharpness services. Here, in the peaceful setting of Sharpness station, No.1444 glints in the fading light of an autumn afternoon as it awaits departure with the 6.00pm service to Berkeley Road on 10th October 1964. This was the principal intermediate station on the east bank of the river Severn of the former Severn & Wye Joint Railway that was operated by the GWR and MR companies. Latterly, the line connected Berkeley Road and Lydney Town stations a distance of nine miles which, of course, involved crossing the river Severn so the short journey was not without interest. Disaster struck, however, on the night of 25th October 1960 when two oil barges *en route* from Avonmouth to Gloucester missed the entrance to Sharpness locks and drifted up the Severn in thick fog. They grazed a pier of the railway bridge causing two spans to collapse and strike the barges which exploded and caught fire, thus severing the line across the river. BR immediately arranged a shuttle service on the eastern section of the severed route between Berkeley Road and Sharpness but by the summer 1961 timetable this had been reduced to little more than a workmen's service with no trains during the middle part of the day. The accident had clearly sealed the fate of this line and passenger trains were withdrawn from 2nd November 1964, thus rendering Gloucester shed's allocation of 1400 Class engines redundant, the Chalford service finishing at the same time. *Tim Stephens*

An unidentified inter-regional working crosses over to the Bristol route at Standish Junction, outside Gloucester, in the early 1960s. Motive power is provided by former GWR 'Castle' Class 4-6-0 No.7001 *Sir James Milne* which is in rather dirty condition. The vast majority of these engines were naturally named after castles but there were exceptions, as seen here. No.7001 was out-shopped from Swindon in May 1946 and lasted in service until September 1963. Note that the coach formed immediately behind the locomotive has been equipped with B4 bogies that were starting to come on stream at that time. This type of bogie gave a vastly improved ride compared to the traditional BR Standard bogie they replaced. *Rail Photoprints*

Introduced in 1932 for light branch line work the 1400 Class 0-4-2Ts (formerly Class 4800) were found all over the former WR system, very often powering pull-push trains; the 5800 Class engines were virtually identical but not pull-push fitted. A total of 75 of these small but attractive 1400 Class locomotives was constructed during a four-year period. The class remained intact until the mid-1950s when branch line closures started to take their toll and by the end of that decade more than half of the class had been sent to the scrapheap. The year 1964 was destined to be the class's last full year in traffic and most examples were based at Gloucester shed for working the Chalford and Sharpness motor trains. In its closing years the class was particularly associated with the Gloucester to Chalford pull-push service along the Golden Valley which served no fewer than 12 stations or halts in 16 miles and had the atmosphere of a branch line despite the fact that the trains operated along the Gloucester to Swindon main line. In this picture No.1458 is depicted working the 9.30am Chalford to Gloucester Central service near St. Mary's Crossing Halt on 29th September 1964. The steam rail motor service was originally introduced on this section by the GWR in 1903, so it really was the end of an era when the last local train ran up the valley on 31st October 1964 and it is recorded that No.1458 was one of the locomotives in use on that day. *Tim Stephens*

A smoky departure. Stanier 'Jubilee' Class 4-6-0 No.45564 *New South Wales* makes an energetic exit from Gloucester (Eastgate) station with the Sunday 4.45pm Bristol (Temple Meads) to Bradford (Forster Square) express on 17th June 1962. In the 1961 summer timetable this train was advertised as conveying through carriages from Truro (dep.10.50am) and also included a restaurant car from there to Bristol; the arrival time in Bradford was quoted as 11.25pm. Gloucester Eastgate was the former Midland Railway station in the city while Central was previously the Great Western station. In the 1970s BR decided that they could no longer afford the luxury of two stations virtually side-by-side and it was decided to concentrate all services on the latter, this, of course, benefiting passengers changing trains who would no longer have to walk between the two stations. Gloucester Eastgate station was closed from 1st December 1975 from which date its remaining services were transferred to the neighbouring Central station. *Martin Smith*

The former station at Titley Junction is seen in this picture which was taken on 6th May 1956, just over a year after the line was closed to passenger traffic; four routes fanned out from this spot which was located in the middle of idyllic Herefordshire countryside. The first line to be built linked Titley with Leominster, on the Shrewsbury to Hereford main line, in the east and the town of Kington in the west. This was proposed in 1853 by a local concern and received the Royal Assent during the following year; the line was opened on 28th July 1857. The railway was later extended beyond Kington to New Radnor, this section opening on 26th September 1875, and the highly optimistic railway pioneers of the day envisaged continuing across Wales to Aberystwyth but nothing came of this fanciful idea. Branches southwards from Titley to Eardisley, on the Hereford to Brecon line, and northwards to the small town of Presteigne, just over the Welsh border, were opened in the 1870s. The Great Western Railway took over all of these lines from 1st July 1887. The routes in this predominantly rural and sparsely populated area were vulnerable to competition from buses and the first line to succumb was the branch to Eardisley which closed from 1st July 1940, a rare example of a railway line being closed during the Second World War. The line to New Radnor was cut back to Kington from 5th February 1951 and four months later passenger trains ran on the Presteigne branch for the last time, the official closure date being 4th June 1951. Finally, the remaining service from Kington to Leominster was withdrawn from 7th February 1955. Titley Junction station seems to be have been well maintained following closure and looks very neat and tidy in this shot; it remains in excellent condition and has since been enhanced by a small railway museum. *Stuart Ackley collection*

A shot taken at the former Kington station on 10th September 1964 showing Collett 1400 Class 0-4-2T No.1420 undertaking a little light shunting; note the shunter is carrying his pole in the traditional manner. In more prosperous times the station here was reputed to have a staff of twenty but the steady decline in the line's fortunes is illustrated by the fact that the service to Presteigne was down to three trains a day by 1939. After the withdrawal of the passenger trains in the 1950s, as previously mentioned, both Kington and Presteigne retained their goods services until 28th September 1964, a few weeks after this portrait was taken. The shunter would not be needing his pole for much longer. *Roy Denison*

A HEREFORDSHIRE BYWAY

A momentous event in the run-down of steam traction on BR occurred on 11th June 1965 when 'Castle' Class 4-6-0 No.7029 *Clun Castle* was turned out to work the last scheduled steam train from Paddington, the 4.15pm to Banbury. The locomotive, which is seen here at Bicester, was in very presentable condition with its copper capped chimney and safety valve bonnet gleaming in the best traditions of the GWR and to add to the occasion it displayed the train identification number on the front of its smokebox. Appropriately for such a historic occasion, the departure took place amidst much television and press publicity. No.7029 put up quite an impressive performance, covering the 18¾ miles from Princes Risborough to Bicester in even time, 18mins 50sec start to stop, with a maximum speed of 82mph at Blackthorn. The following day *Clun Castle* was again in action, but this time out of the limelight working an excursion from Cheltenham to Weston-super-Mare and after taking the empty stock to Bridgwater it penetrated further into the West Country by running 'light engine' to Taunton for servicing. Three other 'Castles' were theoretically still in service in mid-June 1965, including Nos.5042 *Winchester Castle* and 7034 *Ince Castle*, both of which were employed on parcels and goods duties, but No.7022 *Hereford Castle* was reportedly stored at Gloucester. *Rail Photoprints*

The branch from Cheddington to Aylesbury High Street, which was opened as early as 1839 by the Aylesbury Railway, was sometimes said to be the first branch line in the world. It was operated by the London & Birmingham Railway and later by the LNWR who subsequently absorbed the local company. The branch was independent in character and did not link with any other line at the Aylesbury end which may have been a factor in its demise, the passenger trains ceasing from 2nd February 1953. Goods workings continued, however, for a further ten years until they, too, ended on 2nd December 1963. There is still frost on the sleepers as Stanier Class 8F 2-8-0 No.48729 makes its way gingerly along the branch towards the former High Street station with a coal train on Christmas Eve 1962. *Tommy Tomalin*

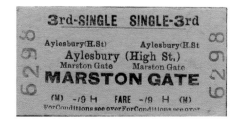

The old Birmingham (New Street) station consisted of the Midland Railway platforms on one side of the premises, these being separated from LNWR platforms on the other side by a public road. The LNWR part of the station was originally under an overall roof but this was destroyed by German bombers during the Second World War and replaced by individual awnings which gave some parts of this side of the station a rather claustrophobic feel. The short platforms were a hindrance to the operating authorities for whom the modernisation of the premises made life much easier, but the rebuilt station certainly had its critics and was seen as a mixed blessing by many travellers. In this portrait, which dates from the early 1960s, former LMS Rebuilt 'Patriot' 4-6-0 No.45534 *E. Tootal Broadhurst* is seen on the former LNWR side at the London end of the station. *RCTS Archive*

Railway historians generally agree that the run-down of the Great Central Line (GC) can be traced back to 1st February 1958 when administration of the line was transferred from the Eastern Region to the London Midland Region of BR. The line was the 'London Extension' of the Manchester Sheffield & Lincolnshire Railway and opened on 15th March 1899, but most of the larger traffic centres along the route already had direct services to London and it had the additional handicap of passing through a thinly populated rural part of central England between Aylesbury and Rugby. BR was in financial difficulties throughout the 1950s and was seeking economies, part of which was the elimination of what were perceived to be duplicate routes. Inter-regional rivalries are thought to have played a part in the downfall of the GC line and there is no doubt that the LMR soon got to work on reducing the route's status, the first blow being struck in January 1960 when the through Marylebone to Manchester expresses were withdrawn. The next substantial landmarks in the decline of the GC line occurred from 4th March 1963 when local trains between Aylesbury and Sheffield ceased, apart from those between Rugby and Nottingham which were retained for workpeople. Sunday trains north of Aylesbury, which had been well patronised, no longer ran after 10th March. Three weekday, mainly steam-worked semi-fast services between Marylebone and Nottingham survived the onslaught plus miscellaneous cross-country and overnight passenger workings but it is arguable whether they contributed materially to the service. When the line's very heavy through goods traffic was switched to other lines in June 1965 there could be no doubting BR's intention to close the route. The end came for the GC line as a through route on 5th September 1966 when the line between Aylesbury and Rugby (Central) was officially closed. Here, BR Standard Class 5MT No.73010 gets into its stride north of Aylesbury with the four-coach 4.38pm *ex*-Marylebone on 25th April 1964. *Tommy Tomalin*

Leicester City and Manchester United contested the 1963 Cup Final, which was played at Wembley Stadium on 25th May. A series of special trains for Leicester supporters, routed via the GC line, was provided and local BR staff entered into the spirit of the occasion by ensuring that as many locomotives as possible were turned out in exemplary condition. Many of the football extras left Leicester quite early and produced a real treat for lineside observers who were able to photograph a procession of southbound workings in ideal early morning sunshine and, for a change, some of the locomotives were really clean. Here, shining LMS 'Jubilee' Class 6P5F No.45598 *Basutoland* picks up water from Charwelton troughs on its way south. *Tommy Tomalin*

The GC line was famous for its dense goods traffic, many trains being Annesley to Woodford Halse coal workings, which were known as 'runners' or 'windcutters'. Latterly, most of these trains were hauled by BR Standard Class 9F 2-10-0s, of which no fewer than 30 examples were based at Annesley in 1962 and here one of that depot's stud, No.92095, hurries southwards through Charwelton on 25th May 1963. The seven miles between Braunston and Charwelton were graded 1 in 176 against southbound trains so the firemen would have had their work cut out, but from Charwelton to Aylesbury the grades were generally in favour of southbound trains. *Tommy Tomalin*

A breath of fresh air at last. The fireman of BR Standard Class 9F No.92069 leans from the cab of the locomotive, perhaps gasping for fresh air after threading the smoky bore of Catesby tunnel with a southbound coal train also on 25th May 1963. The tunnel was over a mile long and southbound trains, as previously mentioned, faced a rising gradient of 1 in 176. An estimated 30 million bricks were apparently used in its construction and the contractors completed the work in just over two years. It is open to question whether a tunnel was necessary at all: a cutting would have been feasible, and it was reputedly built at the behest of a local landowner who presumably did not want to have trains spoiling his view. Nearby is historic Catesby House, a remote hideaway which was one of the meeting places used by the conspirators who hatched the Gunpowder Plot. *Tommy Tomalin*

Prior to the GC line's takeover by the LMR in 1958 Gresley Class A3 Pacifics, supplemented by Class V2 2-6-2s, were an everyday sight on the route's expresses while goods traffic was largely handled by a variety of former LNER classes including class O1 and O4 2-8-0s and Class K3 2-6-0s. Another class that was very common on goods workings were the WD 2-8-0s, of which Woodford Halse shed had 25 on its books in mid-1962. The Class B1 4-6-0s were also regularly diagrammed on the less arduous passenger duties and in this shot No.61111 is seen working a local train near Tibshelf, between Nottingham and Sheffield, in the early 1960s. So, during that period the GC line retained very much an LNER atmosphere but this was diluted as former LMS locomotive types were drafted in by the LMR. *RCTS Archive*

Maroon station signs, a traditional W. H. Smith bookstall, at least two members of the station staff in attendance on the platform and a selection of barrows tidily stored out of the way that would be considered collectors' items today. There is no doubt that Melton Mowbray Town station seemed reasonably busy when this shot was taken of BR Standard Class 4MT No.75042 coming to a halt with the Saturdays only 8.45am Leicester London Road to Peterborough East train on 4th August 1962. The equivalent train in the 1963 summer timetable was the 8.55am from Leicester which was allowed almost two hours to cover the 52¾ miles between the two cities. Both platforms have decorative canopies and supporting stanchions so passengers were well protected from the elements and need not have worried during wet weather. In the distance, on the right of the shot, part of the signal box can just be discerned; rather strangely the box is known officially as 'Melton Station'. This area is still semaphore signalled at the time of writing. *Tommy Tomalin*

Oh, we do like to be beside the seaside! In the 1950s and early 1960s most British families took their holiday at a traditional resort and many went by train as car ownership was not as widespread as it is today. The timing of the annual 'getaway' was determined to a large degree by the dates of the school holidays and consequently huge numbers of people were on the move during the peak months of July and August when, in theory at least, the fickle British weather was at its best. This mass exodus placed an enormous strain on the railway's resources and, as a result, virtually every available passenger coach and serviceable locomotive was pressed into service to meet the demands of holiday-makers. The resort of Great Yarmouth was a favourite with those living in the East Midlands and on summer Saturdays the principal stations were thronged with excited people looking forward to their annual fortnight by the sea. In this picture Class 4F 0-6-0 No.44403, powering the 9.12am SO Leicester to Yarmouth Vauxhall train, leaves a magnificent smokescreen over the Leicestershire countryside as it accelerates away from its Melton Mowbray station stop on 4th August 1962. During the Beeching era this sort of seasonal traffic, for which little-used coaches were retained throughout the year, was identified as totally uneconomic and workings such as this quickly disappeared from the timetables. *Tommy Tomalin*

Photographed on the same day as the previous picture, BR Standard Class 5MT No.73135 rushes over Melton Mowbray water troughs with the 10.00am SO King's Norton to Yarmouth Vauxhall holiday extra. This locomotive, which was based at Derby shed at the time of this picture, was one of 30 members of this class fitted with Caprotti valve gear. *Tommy Tomalin*

Many railway routes offer photographers some high vantage points where the landscape can be included, thus adding more appeal to a picture, but the immediate area around Melton Mowbray has no such opportunities. The intrepid photographer was, therefore, obliged to climb the water tank serving the troughs to gain height and was rewarded with this shot of the 11.00am Yarmouth to Leicester London Road train steaming sedately along with a pair of former LMS Class 4F 0-6-0s, Nos.44113 and 44403, at its head. Brentingby Junction signal box can just be discerned beyond the road overbridge in the background. This was No.44403's second appearance of the day which suggests that it worked as far as Peterborough East and no doubt the crew wouldn't have been too enthusiastic about taking their steed right through to Yarmouth! While the beach at Great Yarmouth no doubt had its attractions it is debatable whether they exceeded those of Melton Mowbray water troughs on a sunny day with a passenger train hauled by double-headed 4Fs! What more could one ask for?
Tommy Tomalin

Another train heading for Yarmouth passes the lovely old Midland Railway Brentingby Junction signal box, about 2 miles east of Melton Mowbray, with Stanier 'Black Five' 4-6-0 No.45285 in charge on 4th August 1962. This particular working was the 10.05am from Derby and the photographer recorded that it passed his vantage point at 11.10am. Note the outline of the signalman in classic pose inside the signal box. This section of line was opened to goods traffic from 1st November 1879, local passenger workings from 2nd February 1880, while through passenger services from London to Nottingham started running from 1st June 1880. *Tommy Tomalin*

The early railway entrepreneurs were nothing if not unrestrained optimists and their expectations were certainly not fulfilled in the case of the Leicester Belgrave Road branch. Opened by the Great Northern Railway (GNR) on 2nd October 1882, there were services to Grantham and Peterborough, but both routes were completely rural in character and prospects were not very promising. The Peterborough trains were withdrawn as early as 1st April 1916 but the service to Grantham, which consisted of five weekday trains each way daily, remained largely unchanged until about 1950, by which time it had dwindled to two trains. When regular passenger services over the joint line were earmarked for withdrawal in 1952 (and implemented from 7th December 1953) it was intended that the meagre weekday timetable along the Belgrave Road branch would cease at the same time, but all attempts to entice the local bus company to provide an alternative means of transport failed and workmen's services continued until 27th April 1957. Thereafter, Belgrave Road station, which boasted a spacious concourse and six platforms, was used only by excursion trains for a relatively brief period during the summer with Skegness being by far the most popular destination. In this very rare colour photograph of the station, taken on 21st July 1962, smoke blows around doing its best to frustrate the photographer; the trains in view are the 8.55am SO to Skegness with B1 Class No.61175 in charge and the 9.10am to Mablethorpe with sister locomotive No.61361 at its head. Belgrave Road station closed its doors for the last time on 9th September 1962 when the final seaside excursion trains ran. *Tommy Tomalin*

The location depicted here is Humberstone station in the Leicester suburbs which is not to be confused with Humberstone Road station on the Midland main line, a short distance away. The delightful somersault signal, vintage oil lamp and rather rickety-looking platform surface, not to mention the weather-beaten station nameboard, all combine to make a real gem of a photograph. Remarkably, there is even a train in this picture, this being one of the workings seen in the previous shot, although with only three advertised trains per week in each direction in the 1959 timetable railway photographers really had to do their homework if they wanted a train to complete the scene. There were two trains on a Saturday morning with one on Sunday mornings until the end of the summer timetable on 13th September. The journey time to Skegness was about 2¾ hours, this being inflated by various speed restrictions due to the poor condition of the track on some stretches of line. In 1959 the Sunday train left Belgrave Road at 9.45am and the return working from Skegness departed at 7.34pm, the arrival time back in Leicester being rather late at 10.21pm so it was not the ideal day out for young children. Perhaps the departure time from the coast was determined by the opening times of the local fish and chip establishments! *Tommy Tomalin*

Following the cessation of the workmen's trains in 1957 Belgrave Road, Humberstone, Thurnby & Scraptoft, and Melton Mowbray North stations all remained open for the summer-only seaside excursions and in this picture B1 Class No.61361, in commendably sparkling condition, is seen about a mile east of Thurnby & Scraptoft station. Fast running was precluded by the bad state of the permanent way, this being exemplified by the fact that 29 minutes were allowed to cover the 14¾ miles between Thurnby & Scraptoft and Melton Mowbray. This picture was also taken on 21st July 1962. Judging by the clouds the photographer appears to have been lucky to have the sun shining at just the right moment. *Tommy Tomalin*

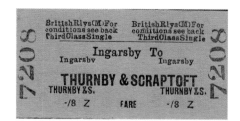

The East Coast Main Line is well known as a racing ground for Sir Nigel Gresley's thoroughbred Pacifics but in steam days it carried a wide variety of traffic powered by a multiplicity of locomotive types. In this picture, taken just north of Huntingdon North station on Sunday 17th June 1962, a Class 9F appears at first sight to be overtaking Gresley Class A4 Pacific No.60006 *Sir Ralph Wedgwood* which was powering an express bound for King's Cross. In reality, No.92186 was reversing slowly along the up fast line during re-ballasting operations so this shot is somewhat deceptive to say the least. The section of track immediately in front of the Class 9F does not seem to have been re-ballasted at all so let's hope the permanent way staff had everything under control and it was ready for the Monday morning. *Tommy Tomalin*

In this illustration, a northbound express is depicted in soft evening sunshine just north of the site of the former Abbots Ripton station which served a small community and was closed from 15th September 1958. Motive power is provided by Gresley Class A3 Pacific No.60046 *Diamond Jubilee* and this picture was also taken on 17th June 1962. The site of the station and signal box is just visible in the background. Note the formation of the train, the first three vehicles immediately behind the locomotive being of Gresley, BR Standard and Thompson design respectively. Regrettably, *Diamond Jubilee* was in its last full year of service being withdrawn exactly a year after this shot was taken. *Tommy Tomalin*

Change at Holme for Ramsey. The former Great Northern branch to Ramsey lost its passenger trains from 6th October 1947 but Holme staved off closure until 6th April 1959. In this picture, taken on 29th September 1962, WD Class 2-8-0 No.90613 has just passed the site of Holme station and is passing over the secondary road at the south end of the former premises, the level crossing being under the control of the adjacent signal box. Note that there appear to be two sets of gates operated independently. No.90613 was one of 934 of these robust and workmanlike 2-8-0s built by the North British Locomotive Co. and Vulcan Foundry as part of the war effort from 1943 onwards; this particular example was constructed by the latter and entered service in January 1944. Steam is being emitted by Ivatt Class 4MT 2-6-0 No.43082 which is waiting in the background for the goods train to pass. *Tommy Tomalin*

Sir Nigel Gresley will always be associated with his legendary Pacifics but, perhaps, he should really be remembered for his V2 Class 2-6-2 locomotives, sometimes described as 'the engines that helped win the war' due to their incredible haulage capability. They certainly proved indispensable when it came to keeping traffic moving along the East Coast Main Line in difficult wartime conditions. During the period from June 1936 to July 1944 a total of 184 examples were built for mixed traffic use. Here, No.60841 is in full cry as it approaches Holme in charge of a southbound goods on 29th September 1962. The author will always remember a stirring run behind sister engine No.60919 on the 6.00pm Aberdeen to Glasgow Buchanan Street in August 1965. That was a heavy Sunday evening train and the locomotive produced a wonderful staccato noise as it surmounted the various summits between the Granite City and Dundee where a diesel was booked to take over – a steam run that will never be forgotten. The Ramsey branch, which was presumably still open for goods traffic at that time, veers off to the right; note the vintage somersault signal. *Tommy Tomalin*

The landscape between Huntingdon and Peterborough is rather bleak and featureless but just north of Holme there is an area of woodland which does offer some relief from the monotony. Here, Gresley Class A3 No.60107 *Royal Lancer* is seen heading south at Holme Lode where the line crosses a minor road to a farm. This machine entered service in May 1923 and lasted in traffic until September 1963. The withdrawal in December 1962 of five Class A4s based at King's Cross shed presaged the end of steam on the East Coast Main Line and in June 1963 steam traction was officially banned south of Hitchin, when the celebrated motive power depot at King's Cross was closed and its remaining Pacifics moved to Peterborough. The final recorded appearance of an A4 at King's Cross station in ordinary service was on 29th October 1963 but such was the chronic unreliability of the diesel fleet no fewer that forty steam visitors were recorded there in December 1963 alone. The last A4s in England were either withdrawn or transferred to Scotland in October 1963 but the A3s fared a little better and seven locomotives remained on the books in England until late 1964 when they were taken out of service, leaving just three survivors north of the border. No.60112 *St Simon* made what is thought to have been the final visit of a Gresley Pacific in ordinary service to the London area when it worked an empty coaching stock train to Hornsey on 12th November 1964. *Tommy Tomalin*

A grimy Thompson Class B1 4-6-0, No.61061, ambles along the up slow line at Little Bytham with a lengthy goods working in tow. The first B1 Class engine appeared from Darlington Works in December 1942 and the locomotives were produced over a long period, the last example to enter traffic being No.61399 in April 1952; a total of 410 were built. The majority of the locomotives were built by the North British Locomotive Co. in Glasgow but some were also constructed by Vulcan Foundry while Gorton Works also produced a small number. The first 40 engines numerically, which were largely named after species of antelope, were among the various batches built at Darlington while other miscellaneous locomotives also carried names. *Tommy Tomalin*

In steam days Grantham was quite an interesting railway centre although it was far from being the largest on the East Coast Main Line (ECML). The 1960 summer timetable advertised an irregular, but reasonably frequent, cross-country service to Derby (Friargate) via Nottingham (Victoria) and the service to Boston via Sleaford amounted to around half-a-dozen weekday trains, but there were none on Sundays. The line to Lincoln (Central) was still in operation and offered about a dozen diesel trains each way on weekdays only, but many of the intermediate stations were not considered sufficiently important to merit a regular service throughout the day and were served only at peak times, presumably to cater for schoolchildren and workpeople. The main focus at Grantham, however, was on the ECML where Sir Nigel Gresley's legendary Pacifics still held sway at that time and there were still some months to go before the introduction of the production series 'Deltics' which changed the face of the ECML so dramatically. The first of those machines took to the rails in early 1961 and no doubt mindful that the dominance of steam traction was about to be severely challenged the photographer visited the Grantham area and took a few pictures that provide a snapshot of the ECML steam fleet. Grantham shed had an allocation of Class A3 Pacifics in 1961 and these included No.60048 *Doncaster* seen here in charge of a London-bound train, also on 23rd May 1961. No.60048 entered service as long ago as August 1924 and remained active until withdrawn in September 1963. *Tony Sullivan*

There was a motive power depot at Grantham and the station's status as an engine changing point meant that the shed had an allocation of Pacifics which in 1961 totalled thirteen Class A3 locomotives. In this portrait, taken on 23rd May 1961, spring flowers add interest to the picture as Peppercorn Class A1 Pacific No.60154 *Bon Accord* leaves Peascliffe tunnel with a London-bound express. The A1 Class locomotives were said to be rough riders but were excellent locomotives in every other respect, being free steamers, and they required less maintenance than other classes employed on similar work – a real bonus for shed staff. No.60154 was one of only five examples of the class fitted with roller bearings. *Tony Sullivan*

Needless to say, the streamlined Gresley Class A4 Pacifics had a huge following among the train spotting fraternity along the length of the ECML and seemed to be everyone's favourite class, after all not many engines had such a melodious chime whistle. The A4s based in England were allocated to King's Cross and Gateshead sheds while Haymarket motive power depot in Edinburgh also had a number on its books. Much to the frustration of spotters south of Newcastle-upon-Tyne who could not afford the fare to Newcastle, some of the Haymarket-based locomotives were rarely seen on the southernmost stretches of the ECML. Here, No.60018 *Sparrow Hawk*, which was allocated to Gateshead, pauses at Grantham station with a southbound express on the same day that the previous picture was taken. Following their displacement from the ECML a number of these locomotives were transferred to Scotland for use on the Glasgow to Aberdeen three hour trains but *Sparrow Hawk* was not one of the lucky ones, being withdrawn from traffic in June 1963. *Tony Sullivan*

Applying the finishing touches. Trainspotters visiting locomotive works were often frustrated to see engines in the erecting shop bereft of any identification, apart from an undecipherable chalked number, and sometimes were angered to find a partially complete locomotive with different numbers painted on its cabsides – a spotter's worst nightmare. If the truth was known works were probably much more interested in meeting production targets than ensuring that all of the components from a particular locomotive were kept together. It is, therefore, very likely that the locomotive seen here comprised components from various sister engines and little of the original remained, but the workshop staff weren't too worried so long as it all worked. This shot of an *ex-*works Stanier Class 5MT apparently having its running number painted on the cabside was taken at Crewe works on 27th August 1961 but the actual identity of the engine will forever remain a mystery. Now if it had been fitted with Stephenson valve gear that would have been a giveaway! *Tommy Tomalin*

The last steam locomotive in BR stock to be repaired at Crewe works was BR Standard 'Britannia' Pacific No.70013 *Oliver Cromwell* which was released from shops on 2nd February 1967 – truly the end of a glorious era. The locomotive had been repainted in lined green but reportedly its left hand side nameplate was missing. One of its first duties was to work the 11.45pm Crewe to Preston parcels on 4th February, returning on the 5.35am Preston to Crewe 'local' the following morning, neither of which train should have taxed the Pacific unduly. No.70013 returned to its home shed of Carlisle (Kingmoor) where all of the surviving 'Britannias' had been concentrated as steam was progressively eliminated from other regions. Steam was due to finish in the Carlisle area at the end of December 1967 and *Oliver Cromwell* was selected to haul Kingmoor shed's unofficial 'farewell to steam' special, a 13-coach football excursion to Blackpool on Boxing Day. A party of enthusiasts cleaned the engine overnight and it must have presented a truly memorable sight as it awaited departure from Carlisle;

the train had reportedly been 'timed' for a diesel but No.70013 was only five minutes late into Blackpool South. The return journey was full of incident with No.70013 apparently stalling near Todd Lane Junction and Grayrigg summit being topped at 20mph without assistance, but the fun and games really began at Tebay. The locomotive took water while the fireman went to the shed to request a banker but found the place to be deserted with no engines in steam. He returned to the train ashen faced so the crew bravely decided that, rather than block the West Coast Main Line for hours, they would take the train over Shap without assistance. This proved to be *Oliver Cromwell*'s finest hour and accompanied by a deafening blast from its chimney it surmounted the bank and topped the summit at around 10mph. The author well remembers alighting at Penrith and standing on the platform as No.70013 disappeared into the darkness, such a stirring sight and sound never to be experienced again at that location, apart from 'artificial' rail tours. The following day *Oliver Cromwell* took the 8.05am Carlisle to Manchester (Red Bank Sidings) parcels train and on 30th December worked the 3.15am Hunslet to Carlisle goods. This photograph was taken at Crewe in the mid-1960s. *RCTS Archive*

Whoosh! Stanier Class 5MT 4-6-0 No.45391 overdoes it on Moore troughs, south of Warrington, and the result is a superb action shot for the photographer who was, hopefully, clad from head to toe in reputable oilskins at the time. The fireman really deserved every congratulation: in addition to the spectacular overflow the engine is also belching black smoke and 'blowing off' at the same time, so well done, an excellently choreographed performance. The force of gravity was always 'number one' consideration when locations for water troughs were being selected: after all, if the ground wasn't perfectly level the water would soon trickle down to one end and be lost. The West Coast Main Line from Crewe descends at 1 in 567 just before it reaches the troughs and, after just half a mile on the level, ascends at 1 in 135 towards Acton Grange Junction so the position of the troughs had been cleverly pin-pointed. This picture was taken in June 1965. *Rail Photoprints*

A head for heights. A bird's-eye view from the top of the coaling plant at Patricroft shed, looking eastwards one day in 1964 – it was a precarious but very rewarding vantage point. The depot was located on the Manchester to Liverpool via Earlestown line which crosses the notorious Chat Moss. Whilst it is not apparent from the picture Patricroft shed was particularly interesting because it consisted of two separate shed buildings at right angles to each other, the building on the left of the shot being the more recently built of the two. The shed's turntable is visible in the bottom of the picture together with the ash pits in the middle. This area is steeped in transport history, the world's first long-distance passenger line passed through here and when BR ran a commemorative special to mark the end of steam traction in August 1968 it passed through Patricroft. The historic Bridgewater and Manchester Ship Canals were not far away while the National Coal Board's (NCB) Walkden system was also nearby. That system had more track-work in the area than BR and boasted a workshop at Walkden where NCB locomotives were overhauled. *Rail Photoprints*

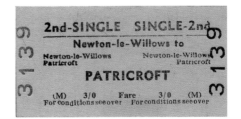

A Lancashire industrial landscape. The line from Kenyon Junction, between Manchester and Earlestown, to Tyldesley was very steeply graded, perhaps a result of severe mining subsidence over the years, and heavy coal trains were banked on a regular basis. This photograph was taken at Jackson's Sidings, just south of Tyldesley, in 1965 and shows BR Standard Class 9F 2-10-0 No.92019 which has just left St. Georges colliery, in the right background. The train is slowly passing Jackson's Sidings signal box and is about to join BR metals for the run to Kenyon Junction. The bridge that carried the Manchester (Exchange) to Wigan (North Western) line is visible to the left of the locomotive. The plume of steam visible above the signal box roof indicates the position of Class 8F No.48636 which had passed on the opposite track a few minutes before this shot was taken. The 8F was assisting a heavily laden, eastbound coal train headed by sister engine No.48491 up the bank towards Tyldesley. Two banking engines were sometimes needed to restart a heavy, loose coupled coal train halted by signals on the bank and one can only imagine the deafening noise produced by three engines working to their absolute limit. *Rail Photoprints*

The large, industrial town of Bolton once boasted two main stations, Trinity Street, on the former L&YR lines from Manchester (Victoria) to Wigan and Preston, and Great Moor Street which was a former LNWR terminal station served purely by local trains. The latter duplicated to some degree services that were available from the neighbouring Trinity Street station and was also easy prey for local buses: it became an early closure victim, closing from 29th March 1954. Trinity Street station consists of two sizeable island platforms from where trains ran to Rochdale via Bury and to Hellifield via Blackburn, in addition to the principal services already mentioned. Regrettably, regular passenger trains to Hellifield ceased from 10th September 1962, but the line remained open throughout and in more recent years regular passenger trains have been re-introduced as far as Clitheroe; in the summer 'Dalesrail' services take ramblers to the Settle & Carlisle line. The Bolton to Rochdale route could be described as an unlucky line because the train service was merely recommended for modification in the Beeching Report, not closure, but the route was apparently added to the list of proposed closures by the London Midland Region (LMR). The line lost its passenger trains from 5th October 1970 and one wonders how the LMR got away with such behaviour! Trinity Street station seems to have been particularly busy when this portrait was taken on a sunny day in 1964. Stanier Class 5MT No.45009 runs through the station non-stop on a train presumably bound for Manchester (Victoria) while a Hughes/Fowler Class 6P5F 2-6-0 No.42708 waits to follow No.45009 once the 'road' ahead is clear. On the left of the shot a non-corridor coach brings up the rear of a westbound train; even as late as 1965 many of these vehicles could still be found on relatively long-distance trains in Lancashire. Note the long platform canopies which provide more than adequate protection from the weather. *RCTS Photo Archive*

Former L&YR Aspinall Class 27 0-6-0 No.52271 enjoys the hospitality of Newton Heath shed on an unknown date, probably sometime in the early 1960s. This locomotive was a member of a huge class that began life in 1889 and examples continued to be built until 1918; the class eventually totalled 468 engines, of which 245 entered BR stock in 1948. This particular engine was constructed at Horwich in December 1894 and lasted in traffic until withdrawn in August 1961. A total of 16 engines survived into 1962, based mainly at Bolton and Lees (Oldham) sheds, but a small fleet was also maintained at Crewe Works for shunting duties; the final survivor was No.52515 which lasted almost until the end of the year. *W. Potter/Kidderminster Railway Museum*

Horwich Locomotive Works had a fleet of five former L&YR 0-6-0 saddle tank locomotives for shunting purposes and the engines, most unusually, retained their LMS numbers upon nationalisation of the railways in 1948. The locomotives were originally L&YR Class 23 0-6-0 tender engines, designed by Barton Wright, and the first example entered traffic in 1877. Many were rebuilt as 0-6-0 saddle tank locomotives in the Aspinall era between 1891 and 1900, and were considerably successful in this form. The curved rear steps, which originally matched the steps on the tender, were the only visible sign that the engines had been rebuilt. The five representatives at Horwich Works were progressively taken out of traffic during the early 1960s, leaving No.11305 as the final survivor and, for a brief period in 1964, this engine had a claim to fame as the oldest working steam locomotive on BR. This picture was taken on 16th September 1962. *Peter Fitton*

Blasting up to the summit. The line between Todmorden (Hall Royd Junction) and Burnley (Gannow Junction) is universally known to enthusiasts as the 'Copy Pit route', taking its name from a small colliery that was located near to the summit. The line was opened by the Lancashire & Yorkshire Railway in November 1849 and is very steeply graded, climbing to a summit at Copy Pit which is 749 feet above sea level. There were various intermediate stations along the route which served small communities but some, such as Cornholme, closed in the 1930s while others survived until the late-1950s and an irregular local passenger service ran between Todmorden and Burnley until November 1965. The line was an important freight artery, however, and also carried considerable seasonal passenger traffic from the West Riding to Blackpool. Towards the end of the steam era as steam traction was eliminated from other routes, the Copy Pit line gained a higher profile as one of the last locations where steam engines could be seen working uphill to their limit. A steady stream of heavy coal trains from Yorkshire to power stations on the other side of the Pennines was a regular feature of the line and these workings needed banking assistance up the 1 in 65 incline from Stansfield Hall (Todmorden) to the summit. In this shot a westbound coal train is seen approaching Copy Pit summit on 18th May 1968 with two groups of photographers, one on each side of the line, recording the scene for posterity as Stanier Class 8F 2-8-0s Nos.48410 and 48519 exert maximum effort on the climb. Sadly, during this period locomotives that were star performers on one day could suffer a relatively minor defect and find themselves cast aside to the scrap line the following day. *David Rodgers*

In the 1960s before the advent of cheap continental holidays, BR used to run many 'Saturdays Only' trains to resorts for the benefit of holiday-makers spending their annual fortnight by the sea and many of these trains were steam-powered. During the winter months there was very little steam activity on passenger trains between Leeds and Manchester but on summer Saturdays steam staged a resurgence. On Saturday mornings a trio of trains from Manchester (Exchange) to Scarborough, Filey Holiday Camp and Newcastle-upon-Tyne were booked for steam usually using BR Standard Class 5MTs from Patricroft shed; the locomotives later returned home on the corresponding return workings. The 11.25am SO Newcastle-upon-Tyne to Llandudno usually produced a Stanier Class 5MT but on 8th July 1967 'Jubilee' No.45593 *Kolhapur* unexpectedly appeared and was photographed crossing Longwood viaduct. Later in the summer *Kolhapur*, one of the last surviving 'Jubilees', made regular sorties over the Settle & Carlisle line on dated Saturday trains that were well patronised by enthusiasts and No.45593 subsequently survived into preservation. *David Rodgers*

The 4th of November 1967 dawned bitterly cold and cloudless in the West Riding after a heavy overnight frost – perfect conditions for steam railway photography. In this illustration Stanier Class 5MT No.44983 is seen, to quote the photographer, 'on its hands and knees' as it heaves a heavy coal train up the 1 in 105 gradient between Huddersfield and Standedge tunnel. The 'Black Five' was making desperately slow progress, slipping and sliding on the greasy rails, and it is seen here between Longwood & Milnsbridge and Golcar.
David Rodgers

The LMS constructed a huge fleet of 645 Class 4MT 2-6-4Ts for suburban and stopping services during a long 20-year period from 1927, with the last examples being built under BR jurisdiction in 1951. This massive fleet had been whittled down to just a handful of locomotives, of both Stanier and Fairburn designs, by the autumn of 1967 all based at sheds in the West Riding for local passenger duties. Those turns included powering the Bradford portions of King's Cross expresses between there and Leeds but in this portrait, taken on 8th July 1967, Fairburn-designed No.42073 is seen charging up the 1 in 50 climb from Bradford (Exchange) with the 9.06am to Poole. No.42073 would have worked only to Huddersfield where its short formation would have been attached to the main train which came from Leeds. This machine was built at Brighton in November 1950 and worked on the Southern Region for a time in the 1950s; it was fortunate enough to survive into preservation. On 1st October sister engine No.42152 took the very last steam train from Bradford (Exchange) to Leeds and virtually all Eastern Region steam traction in the area was withdrawn from that date, apart from a stud of Stanier Class 8Fs retained at Royston. *David Rodgers*

Acres of sidings stretching as far as the eye can see, stock in the bay platform and a substantial station building, all providing ample testament to Normanton's once undisputed status as an important railway centre and, of course, there was a motive power depot to provide traction for the dozens of daily coal trains that operated. One must not overlook Class 4F 0-6-0 No.44274, from nearby Royston shed, taking a mixed goods train through the station in this portrait which was taken in May 1963. Normanton was, of course, an important coal mining centre and heavy freight was the railway's primary traffic as evidenced here by the huge marshalling yard. Passenger services were secondary compared to freight but even so it was possible to travel on through trains to London (St Pancras), Liverpool, Manchester and Newcastle-upon-Tyne, and many local destinations. Whatever happened to those days of prosperity?
Martin Smith

The branch from Skipton to Grassington in the Yorkshire Dales lost its passenger trains way back in September 1930, but mineral trains continued to run to a quarry at Swinden and for nearly 40 years the line had a low profile. Towards the end of steam it became clear that the Grassington branch had become the last steam-worked branch in the country and photographers descended on the line to photograph the BR Standard Class 4MTs which were booked to work the trains. Here No.75019, which had been cleaned by enthusiasts at Rose Grove shed, sparkles in the sunshine as it heads towards Skipton in June 1968. *Author*

A panoramic view of the northern approach to Southport station on 23rd July 1960 with a veteran former Lancashire & Yorkshire Railway (L&YR) 2-4-2T No.50850 shuffling around the station area on carriage shunting duties. The engine shed is visible beyond the train and also the signal box which no doubt provided a panoramic view of operations. The L&YR possessed a substantial fleet of these locomotives, a total of 330 being built between 1889 and 1911, of which 109 entered BR stock. The locomotives weighed 59 tons 3 cwt (with variations) and had a tractive effort of 18,955 lb, though it should be noted that some engines were marginally less powerful. By the end of 1960 the class had been reduced to just three examples, Nos.50721, 50746 and 50850, nominally in service at the end of that year but Bank Hall shed's No.50721 was withdrawn in January 1961 leaving just two examples at Southport. They were displaced from their carriage shunting duties there by the arrival of two Ivatt Class 2MT 2-6-2Ts and went into store, and No.50746 was taken out of service shortly afterwards. Miraculously, No.50850 re-entered traffic during the summer and remained the last active survivor until withdrawn in October 1961. This machine entered service from Horwich works as long ago as September 1899 so it certainly had a long innings; a representative of the class is preserved in the National Collection. *Richard S. Greenwood MBE*

Southbound trains from Lancaster (Castle) faced a tricky 1 in 98 gradient which could prove challenging for some locomotives when rail conditions were greasy, making engines prone to slip. In this photograph Hughes/Fowler Class 6P5F 2-6-0 No.42860, hauling a very heavy stone train, appears to be taking the bank in its stride, no doubt helped by the dry weather conditions. It is doubtful whether the locomotive would have been in difficulty even if adhesion was a problem because these engines, universally known as 'Crabs' due to the high running plate and position of the cylinders, were very sure-footed and therefore well-liked by the crews; this photograph was taken in September 1963. Hughes, who was previously with the LYR, was the first Chief Mechanical Engineer of the LMS and responsible for the design of these machines. By the time they were being built he had left office and consequently the fleet of 245 locomotives was built under Fowler's supervision. *Rail Photoprints*

You can almost hear the wheel flanges squealing as an unidentified, grimy Class WD 2-8-0, hauling a train of tank wagons, rounds the very tight curve into Lancaster (Green Ayre) station in October 1965. The train had originated at Heysham and was destined for an industrial installation on Tees-side. The line from Lancaster (Castle), which is also tightly curved, converges from the left while the river Lune can just be discerned on the right of the picture. When this picture was taken Green Ayre station was still relatively busy with a service of frequent electric trains which connected the Lancaster stations with Morecambe and Heysham, but the electric units were non-standard, life expired and this gave BR the ideal pretext to seek withdrawal of this useful local service. In addition to those trains Green Ayre station was also served by Leeds to Morecambe via Skipton workings but both of these services were withdrawn from 3rd January 1966, from which date Green Ayre station was closed with the Leeds trains being diverted to run via Carnforth. *David Mitchell*

During the summer of 1964 nineteen Stanier 'Princess Coronation' Pacifics were still nominally in service although No.46226 *Duchess of Norfolk* was dumped out of use at Carlisle Kingmoor shed with a cracked cylinder. The survivors had largely been relegated to powering dated passenger, van and goods trains by that time but could still be seen on named expresses when the booked diesel locomotive suddenly developed a fault at the last minute, an occurrence that happened with regular monotony. The 4th of September saw the last workings of the 'Caledonian' and, perhaps, it was no coincidence that the final down train was taken by No.46238 *City of Carlisle*: a few days later No.46239 *City of Chester* powered the 11.30am Euston to Carlisle. In this shot No.46240 *City of Coventry* is seen heading northwards in glorious lighting conditions at Morecambe South Junction, just north of Lancaster, with an unidentified train on 24th August 1964. The photographer may not have been aware at the time, but a decision to withdraw almost all of the remaining Stanier Pacifics from 12th September may have already been taken when he took this shot. The West Coast Main Line would never be the same again! *David Mitchell*

2nd-SINGLE   SINGLE-2nd
Hest Bank to
Hest Bank   Hest Bank
Lancaster (Castle)   Lancaster (Castle)
or Carnforth   or Carnforth
LANCASTER (Castle) or
CARNFORTH
(M)   0/5   Fare   0/5   (M)
For conditions see over   For conditions see over

The grime and the glory. The supposed 'romance of the steam age' probably only really existed in the minds of those who never had to work, day in day out, on steam traction. In the middle of winter locomotive crews were said to be almost frozen on one side of their body while the other side was being roasted! It was extremely dirty, laborious and sometimes downright dangerous work and the very often primitive conditions in which the engines were maintained left much to be desired, as exemplified here. Working on steam certainly wasn't the easiest way of earning a living and yet many railwaymen found it a hugely satisfying and rewarding occupation. BR Standard Class 4MT No.75048 had just had its fire dropped when this shot was taken in the gloom of Carnforth shed on 10th July 1968. Any volunteers to clear away the pile of clinker?
David Rodgers

Classic locomotive class, classic location. The afternoon sunshine is reflected off Stanier 'Princess Coronation' Class Pacific No.46252 *City of Leicester* as it heads a portion of the down 'Lakes Express' through the Lune gorge on 18th August 1962. This train divided *en route* on most days and it is likely that by the time it reached this location it consisted of only four or five coaches: perhaps that is why the photographer opted for a 'going away' shot! In the 1963 summer timetable it was scheduled to leave Euston at 11.40am, and conveyed portions to Windermere and Whitehaven (Bransty) via Penrith and Workington (Main). The arrival time at Whitehaven was advertised as 8.08pm and a restaurant car was provided for most of the trip which was probably just as well on such a long journey. When this picture was taken this celebrated class was still intact, but the first condemnations took place at the end of the year and *City of Leicester* was a relatively early casualty, being withdrawn in June 1963. *Gavin Morrison*

In today's more environmentally conscious society it is unlikely that construction of a major motorway through such a tranquil and beautiful area as the Lune Gorge would be sanctioned, but in the 1960s Great Britain was supposedly experiencing a 'technological revolution' and the M6 motorway was probably regarded as 'progress'. The result was that some of the finest railway photographic locations in the country were destroyed and splendid vistas, such as that seen here, were ruined. Here, Stanier Class 5MT 4-6-0 No.44733 takes a southbound goods through the Lune gorge on 18th August 1962. *Gavin Morrison*

The line between Oxenholme and Carlisle has been the scene of some of the finest British steam action photography and looking at this superb study of the Lune gorge it is easy to see why this stretch was such a favourite with photographers. The snow-flecked fells provide a splendid backdrop as an unidentified 'Clan' Pacific heads southwards in November 1964. Today, electrification masts and the intrusive M6 motorway dominate the scene. *David Mitchell*

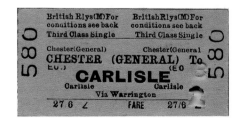

Day in, day out. Enginemen based at Tebay probably had a reasonable variety of turns when the line across the Pennines to Barnard Castle was still in business but by 26th September 1964, when this portrait was taken, much of their time was spent 'commuting' between Tebay and Shap summit on banking engines. Hardly a thrilling job but an absolutely essential one, without which the West Coast Main Line would soon have been brought to a standstill. At least they would have been privileged, if that is quite the appropriate word, to experience the northern fells in all weathers from sunrise to sunset. Fowler Class 4MT 2-6-4T No.42414 has steam to spare as it passes Scout Green giving vigorous rear-end assistance to a northbound freight. *Gavin Morrison*

Shap in the snow. In this picture, taken from an unorthodox angle, Class 5MT 4-6-0 No.44762 clambers up to Shap summit with a northbound van train on 28th November 1964. Note that the formation includes a Royal Mail van, a goods brake van and full brake coach, classified BG for operating purposes. *Gavin Morrison*

Carlisle has always been a rewarding centre for railfans since the arrival of the Newcastle & Carlisle Railway in 1836. That railway did not have the monopoly for long, however, being joined by three other important concerns during the ensuing decade and eventually, after the arrival of the Midland Railway in 1876, no fewer than seven railways operated in the city. One can only imagine the dazzling blaze of colourful liveries! On the debit side it is said that in 1922 there were no fewer than 11 separate goods yards in the city which must have caused endless congestion, and the railway provided employment for many inhabitants. In more recent times Carlisle was fortunate to be one of the last outposts of steam traction and, therefore, one of the most popular destinations for steam enthusiasts. In this picture a Fowler-designed Class 4MT 2-6-4T No.42317 is seen setting off from the Border City in April 1961 with an unidentified train, possibly a local empty stock working. Note the low level goods lines which in former years enabled goods trains from Newcastle and Settle to avoid the main station. The roof of Carlisle station can just be discerned in the middle of the picture. *Rail Photoprints*

One of the last active Stanier 'Jubilee' 4-6-0s on the LMR was No.45627 *Sierra Leone* which was based latterly at Bank Hall shed on Merseyside. In times gone by that depot used to have a small allocation of these engines for working Liverpool Exchange to Newcastle-upon-Tyne services as far as York, and Glasgow trains, a long term resident being No.45719 *Glorious*. In this portrait taken at Carlisle in the mid-1960s *Sierra Leone* is seen leaving with a southbound train, doubtless destined for Liverpool. The locomotive has clearly been spruced up and looks reasonably well cared for compared to other engines at that time. One or two enthusiasts appear to be on board, no doubt hoping for a fast run. *RCTS Archive*

Calamity at Carlisle. A rail tour to mark the imminent withdrawal of the last Gresley Class A3 Pacific was arranged for 5th June 1965. The ranks of the class had been reduced to just three by that date, Nos.60041/52 and 60100, all shedded at St Margarets depot in Edinburgh, so it was logical for the train to start from that city. The train's destination was Carlisle and it was routed outward via Newcastle-upon-Tyne and scheduled to return along the Waverley route back to Edinburgh. The A3 selected to power the train was No.60052 *Prince Palatine* and judging by its sparkling external condition a lot of time had been lavished upon the engine by the depot's cleaners. Alas, the plans went awry after arrival at Carlisle when it was discovered that one of *Prince Palatine*'s axle boxes was running hot and the engine had to be taken out of service. Luckily, another Gresley Pacific, Class A4 No.60027 *Merlin* just happened to be on hand at Kingmoor shed and this was hastily substituted for the disgraced A3 locomotive. *Merlin* was in an extremely dirty condition but was the only suitable engine available and successfully took the modest six-coach train back to Edinburgh without incident. *Rail Photoprints*

Despite the threat of heavy snow across the north of England on 2nd April 1966 it was decided that the Manchester Locomotive Society/Stephenson Locomotive Society 'Lakes & Fells' rail tour would run as advertised. The train left Manchester (Exchange) behind Stanier 'Jubilee' 4-6-0 No.45596 *Bahamas* and that machine powered it as far as Hellifield where Sir Nigel Gresley's celebrated Pacific No.4472 *Flying Scotsman* took over for a run over the frozen wastes of the Settle & Carlisle line and then down to Penrith. The train was already an hour late at Hellifield due to snow clearance operations north of Blackburn. On arrival at Penrith a pair of Ivatt Class 2MT 2-6-0s, Nos.46426 and 46458, were waiting to take the excursionists over the splendid Lakeland route to Workington and it must have been a memorable experience being steam-hauled through such a magnificent landscape blanketed by snow. History was made on the journey because this train was the last steam-worked train to cover the entire Penrith to Workington route, the section west of Keswick being scheduled for closure from 18th April. The rail tour later continued down the Cumbrian coast line to Arnside, the lateness having increased to two hours by that point. The enjoyment of some participants was presumably tempered by the atrocious weather conditions and thoughts of being stranded, so they bailed out there and returned to Manchester by diesel train. The more optimistic participants continued to Hellifield, again with *Flying Scotsman* as motive power, and there *Bahamas* took over for the last stage of the tour back to Manchester where arrival was after midnight. One wonders how much public transport was available to get the excursionists home but at least hardened enthusiasts would have a jolly good tale to tell and, of course, they had travelled over the outstandingly scenic Penrith to Workington line behind steam just before part of the route was closed. *RCTS Archive*

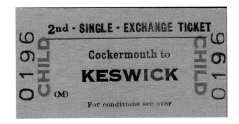

A line without equals. Demanding gradients, inhospitable terrain and a colourful history: few railway routes rival the spectacular Settle & Carlisle line (S&C). The mighty Midland Railway (MR) wanted to run services to Scotland and made overtures to the London & North Western Railway (LNWR) with a view to running through to Carlisle via Ingleton, but the hostile LNWR rejected any possibility of through running forcing the MR to think again. In 1866 the MR proposed a line from Settle to Carlisle and this was sanctioned on 16th July, much to the annoyance of the LNWR which strenuously objected. Having failed to keep its rival out of Carlisle the LNWR moderated its opposition and the MR attempted to abandon the Parliamentary Bill authorising the line, but this angered other railway companies who sought to benefit from the MR's expansion and the MR's bid to abandon the S&C line was rejected by Parliament. The first sod was cut at Anley, near Settle, in November 1869 but construction of the line was bedevilled by disease and drunkeness among the navvies, the atrocious weather conditions and the difficult terrain that sometimes hampered progress for months on end. The MR eventually won through however, the first goods trains running throughout in August 1875 while passenger trains commenced operation on 1st May 1876. The notorious 15 miles-long stretch from Settle Junction to Blea Moor, known to railwaymen as the 'Long Drag', has a 1 in 100 gradient virtually all of the way and was a stern test for any locomotive and its crew. Here, Class WD 2-8-0 No.90595, hauling a heavy coal train, is making very slow progress on the climb as it passes Horton-in-Ribblesdale on 1st March 1960, still with a long way to go to the summit. On this occasion the magnificent Pennine landscape was hidden by mist which at least makes a change from curtains of rain. *Gavin Morrison*

Railway photographers making a pilgrimage to the S&C always knew that much patience, and frequently a bit of luck, would be needed if a decent image was to be obtained. In this photograph much of the moorland behind the train appears to be in shade, but fortunately the train has just entered a welcome patch of sunshine and a memorable shot has resulted. The location is just north of Horton-in-Ribblesdale and the train is the 3.40pm Bradford Forster Square to Carlisle 'all stations' working with Stanier 'Black Five' No.45105 at its head; this photograph was taken on 28th April 1963. The 1963 summer timetable listed two stopping trains each way along the entire length of the S&C line on weekdays with a couple of short workings between Carlisle and Appleby for the benefit of work people and schoolchildren. The train depicted here had a leisurely schedule, which included a 22min. sojourn at Hellifield, presumably to take water, and was booked to arrive in the Border City at 7.29pm. *Gavin Morrison*

On a brilliantly sunny afternoon Stanier 'Jubilee' 4-6-0 No.45593 *Kolhapur* makes steady progress up the final climb to Blea Moor with the relief 'Thames-Clyde Express', the 9.20am St Pancras to Glasgow Central. No.45593 was photographed crossing Ribblehead viaduct on 5th August 1967. The remarkable Indian summer of the 'Jubilee' class in 1967 attracted enthusiasts from far and wide and will be remembered with affection for many years to come. By the date of this photograph only three 'Jubilees' were available to haul the summer Saturday 'extras' over the S&C line but, even so, all the steam turns ran as booked but a 'Britannia', No.70016 *Ariel*, appeared on one of the trains. The train is made up largely of LMS-designed coaches but the formation is marred by the inclusion of a freshly-repainted blue/grey vehicle in the middle. *David Mitchell*

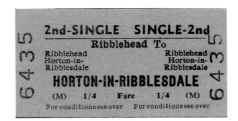

On Saturday 5th August 1967 the S&C route attracted many lineside observers anxious to photograph Holbeck shed's last surviving 'Jubilees' working Anglo-Scottish expresses over this epic line. They had a very welcome, and most unexpected, bonus when former Crosti boiler Class 9F 2-10-0 No.92021 appeared during the afternoon with a long northbound goods train in tow, the 1.30pm Hunslet to Carlisle. There were only a few of these distinctive machines left in service so the visit of No.92021 was particularly fortunate. The locomotive was in appalling external condition but nonetheless made a memorable sight as it approached Dent station in the afternoon sunshine. This picture was taken from a conveniently placed bracket signal which offered a grandstand view of approaching trains and Arten Gill viaduct in the distance. *David Mitchell*

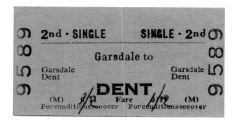

The winter of 1962/63 was particularly harsh in the Yorkshire Dales and passengers travelling on the 10.05pm Edinburgh (Waverley) to London St Pancras train on the night of 19th January 1963 certainly had cause to remember the nightmare journey they suffered. Their train ran into a blizzard near Dent and the snowdrifts forced it to return to Carlisle from where it reportedly reached London via the East Coast Main Line – quite an experience. The S&C route remained blocked for five days and through services were diverted along the West Coast Main Line as far as Low Gill from where they reached Leeds via Ingleton and were then able to take their normal route. The normal motive power arrangements were disrupted and some extremely unusual sightings were made, such as a 'Princess Coronation' Class Pacific on the southbound 'Waverley' on 23rd January and V2 Class No.60802 on the southbound 'Thames-Clyde Express' on 24th January, in each case the trains travelling via Ingleton. The S&C route was reopened on the evening of 24th January and there was subsequently a constant stream of goods trains as efforts were made to clear the backlog of traffic. The ordeal for staff on the line was not over, however, because it was again blocked by snow from 6th to 23rd February when huge drifts accumulated, once again resulting in the diversion of through passenger trains via Low Gill and Ingleton. You can almost feel the cold in this picture of Stanier 'Jubilee' Class 4-6-0 No.45737 *Atlas* picking its way through the snow at Dent station on 26th January 1963, barely 24 hours after the line was reopened. The snow fences on the right were designed to give a modicum of protection to the tracks but they don't seem to have been successful on this occasion. *Gavin Morrison*

Deep snow stretches in all directions as far as the eye can see as a Stanier Class 5MT passes through Dent station with a northbound goods train, also on 26th January 1963. Unsurprisingly, the photographer's Mini appears to have the car park to itself. *David Mitchell*

Deep and crisp and even. The tops of the rails are visible in this portrait taken just south of Rise Hill tunnel on 26th January 1963 but nothing more of the permanent way can be seen, the level of the snow being above rail height. The locomotive is Gresley Class A3 Pacific No.60073 *St Gatien* which was working the southbound 'Waverley'. Interestingly, this machine was based at Heaton shed, Newcastle-upon-Tyne, at the time of the photograph so perhaps it had worked across to Carlisle and been 'borrowed' to haul this train. A truly memorable picture to be sure – how on earth did the photographer managed to keep his fingers sufficiently warm to enable him to press the shutter? Full marks for endurance and dedication. *David Mitchell*

Captured in stunning lighting conditions, BR Standard Pacific No.70006 *Robert Burns* approaches Dent station with a northbound goods train on 18th January 1964. *David Mitchell*

Colour photographs of Class 4F 0-6-0s on the Settle & Carlisle line are uncommon in the author's experience but here is a picture of an unidentified example working a civil engineer's special at Lunds on 29th September 1963. The train is approaching Shotlock Hill tunnel in glorious afternoon sunshine. The lonely Moorcock to Kirkby Stephen road is on the right of the picture while the distinctive outline of Wild Boar Fell dominates the backdrop. The photographer comments that he spent the day following a rail tour around Yorkshire by car, passing through Selby, Harrogate and Skipton in the process before travelling to Towyn for the Talyllyn Railway's Annual General Meeting, so it must have been a day to remember! *David Mitchell*

The reaction of the shed staff at Holbeck motive power depot in Leeds must have been one of shock and disbelief when a batch of Gresley A3 Pacifics was allocated there in 1960 for use on Anglo-Scottish expresses over the Settle & Carlisle route. Holbeck was formerly a Midland Railway shed and came under the LMS following the grouping in 1923 so Gresley locomotives were completely alien. The local crews soon grew to like their new steeds, however, and appreciated their free steaming ability and comfortable cabs. By November 1960 a total of nine Class A3s was based at Holbeck and they put in some excellent work over the demanding Settle line, but their reign was brief because BR/Sulzer Type 4 diesels took over operation of the 'Thames-Clyde Express' from 12th June 1961 and three weeks later ousted the A3s from their other duties, including the 'Waverley' in both directions. The A3s continued to work seasonal and relief trains for some time afterwards, however, and one particular locomotive, No.60038 *Firdaussi*, stayed at Holbeck for a long time after its sister engines had departed, although it was not unknown for Holbeck to borrow A3s from neighbouring Neville Hill shed if the need arose. Here, *Firdaussi* is seen climbing up the final few yards to Ais Gill summit with a relief to the 'Thames-Clyde Express' on 1st September 1962. *Gavin Morrison*

An epic battle. Stanier Class 8F 2-8-0 No.48090 struggles up the last half mile to Ais Gill summit with a heavy train of anhydrite *en route* from Long Meg sidings, near Lazonby, to Widnes; this picture was taken on 4th November 1967, a brilliantly sunny day in the dales following heavy overnight frost. The steam fleet had been subjected to a policy of minimal maintenance for some time and it is debatable whether some locomotives should have been on line work, let alone hauling a heavy long-distance mineral working over the S&C line's demanding 1 in 100 gradients, as seen here. No.48090, which took 45 minutes on the climb from Kirkby Stephen to the summit, emits a volcanic smoke effect as it nears Ais Gill, but vast amounts of steam seem to be escaping at the front end and much of the fireman's endeavour was wasted effort. *Gavin Morrison*

The breathtaking grandeur of the Settle to Carlisle line is seen at its very best in this shot of Stanier Class 8F No.48090 as it makes an agonisingly slow climb up the 1 in 100 towards Birkett tunnel. It was powering a Long Meg to Widnes anhydrite train on a freezing but brilliantly sunny 4th November 1967. The distant outline of the Pennine Chain can just be discerned on the horizon. *David Mitchell*

Sixty of these handsome Class D20 4-4-0s were built between 1899 and 1907 when Wilson Worsdell held the position of Chief Mechanical Engineer of the North Eastern Railway (NER); this is No.62378 which was photographed at York in 1956 shortly before being withdrawn. In the early 1950s the sheds at Tweedmouth and Selby had the largest allocations of these machines. This class was designed to haul the principal expresses between York and Newcastle-upon-Tyne and were the most successful and economical of all the NER's express engines, being preferred by the enginemen to the more powerful Atlantics.
Rail Photoprints

A splendidly clean Gresley Class V2 2-6-2, No.60858, awaits departure from York with (what appears to be) the through Newcastle-upon-Tyne to Colchester train on 14th June 1959. No.60858 was one of five members of this class allocated to March at the time of the photograph which tends to confirm the identity of the train. In the summer 1960 timetable the equivalent of this working was advertised to leave Newcastle at 12.05pm and arrive in Colchester at 8.39pm so it was not exactly one of the Eastern Region's fastest expresses. The train travelled via the Great Northern & Great Eastern Joint Line between Gainsborough and March and served Gainsborough and Lincoln (Central) before running non-stop to March. Following departure from March the train was routed via Bury St Edmunds and Ipswich to Colchester, and a timetable footnote refers to the four separate tables in which the train appears. *Rail Photoprints*

In 1945 when Edward Thompson was the Chief Mechanical Engineer of the LNER No.4470 *Great Northern* (later BR No.60113) was rebuilt as the prototype for his new design of Pacific type locomotives. This engine was substantially rebuilt with three cylinders with divided drive, three separate sets of Walschaert valve gear and an extended wheelbase of 38ft 5ins with 6ft 8in driving wheels. When Thompson retired in 1946 Peppercorn took up office and many of Thompson's ideas were incorporated in his development of the proposed new design including the large remodelled Thompson 118 boiler that had been fitted to his earlier Class A2 Pacifics. In August 1948 the first Class A1 Pacific, No.60114 *W.P. Allen* entered traffic and a total of 49 of these impressive locomotives was built at Doncaster and Darlington in the space of sixteen months. They immediately entered service on the heaviest East Coast Main Line expresses and performed excellently soon gaining a reputation as powerful, sure-footed engines, their Achilles heel being their rough riding tendencies. Another notable advantage of these machines was their reduced maintenance requirement compared to any of the other express passenger locomotives running on BR. In this picture No.60155 *Borderer* is depicted at Northallerton in May 1965, the last full year that this class was in service. *Rail Photoprints*

The short 1½ miles-long branch from Hutton Gate, on the former Middlesbrough to Loftus line, to Guisborough was opened by a local company on 25th February 1854. There was a single platform with an overall roof and the station had the usual facilities such as a goods shed and cattle dock and, perhaps surprisingly for such a small station, there was a locomotive turntable. Operationally the station was a nightmare because through Middlesbrough to Loftus trains had to reverse out while those in the opposite direction had to reverse into the station. The summer 1960 public timetable lists three trains on weekdays only to and from Middlesbrough with an extra service on Saturdays so it was probably not surprising that the branch was tabled for closure in the Beeching Report. The line was closed to passengers from 2nd March 1964 and goods traffic lingered for a few more months until 31st August 1964. In this picture, taken on 3rd May 1958, a commendably clean L1 Class 2-6-4T No.67754 poses at Guisborough station on the last day of through services from Middlesbrough to Scarborough via Loftus. *K. H. Cockerill/ARPT*

Located on the coast line from Newcastle-upon-Tyne to Middlesbrough, Ryhope was an important junction where lines branched off to Ryhope and Silksworth collieries while a route forked in a south-westerly direction towards South Hetton. The last-mentioned line originally continued to Stockton-on-Tees, but passenger trains ceased between Stockton and Wellfield as long ago as November 1931 and other sections of that route subsequently lost their passenger trains on a piecemeal basis. Designed by Raven and introduced in 1913, the Class Q6 0-8-0s were built to handle heavy mineral traffic in the north-east of England and No.63395, seen here at Ryhope in August 1965, was destined to become the last survivor of this 120-strong class. It was built at Darlington entering traffic in December 1918 and never ventured from its native north-east. It was withdrawn from traffic when steam traction was abandoned in that area in September 1967 but fortunately it survived into preservation and, at the time of writing, can be seen at the North Yorkshire Moors Railway, not too far from where it spent almost its entire working life. *Rail Photoprints*

BR's North Eastern Region organised a special train from Newcastle-upon-Tyne to Rothbury which was routed outward via Hexham and returned via Morpeth and the East Coast Main Line. Reportedly called the 'Station Gardens Special', it ran on 14th August 1955 and was hauled by former North Eastern Railway Class J21 No.65103, a real 'old timer' which was built at Gateshead works from where it emerged in February 1892. A total of 201 of these machines was built between 1886 and 1894 of which 83 entered BR stock in 1948, the first withdrawals having occurred in 1929. Remarkably, these engines were once staple motive power over the heavily graded Stainmore route from Barnard Castle to Kirkby Stephen. The title of this train is rather misleading because all of the stations between Reedsmouth and Morpeth, including those on the Rothbury branch, had been closed since 15th September 1952 and presumably some were overrun by weeds by the date of the tour, and were hardly a horticulturist's dream. This must have been a fascinating trip, however, with veteran motive power along some outstandingly scenic lines closed to regular passenger trains; this picture was taken at Corbridge on the first stage of the tour. The line between Newcastle-upon-Tyne and Carlisle was the first linking the west and east coasts in Great Britain and was opened from Carlisle to Gateshead by the Newcastle and Carlisle Railway Company on 18th June 1838, and an extension to Newcastle was brought into use the following year. *Rail Photoprints*

Some of the most arduous duties towards the end of steam were the very heavy iron ore workings from Tyne Dock, near South Shields, to the steelworks at Consett which was situated on the 850ft contour. The iron ore trains were introduced in 1953 following a decision to expand capacity at the works and consisted of block trains of up to eight 56-ton hopper wagons, and initially the workings were handled by Class O1 2-8-0s with Class Q7 0-8-0s assisting at the rear over the most demanding sections. The trains were routed via Boldon colliery and Pelton, and the sight and sound of these extremely heavy workings charging up 1 in 50 gradients with locomotives at each end of the train must have been a truly unforgettable experience. In this shot Class O1 2-8-0 No.63760, which is in reasonably clean condition, is taking the Consett line at South Pelaw Junction, near Chester-le-Street, on a sunny day sometime in 1957. The route in the foreground is the old Stanhope & Tyne line to Consett which required rope working but was still partially in use to serve local collieries. The train has just left the route from Washington, a line closed when the Consett iron ore trains were diverted to run via Gateshead and steam traction on these workings was replaced by diesels. The tracks going off to the left converge with the East Coast Main Line. There used to be a passenger service from Consett to Newcastle-upon-Tyne via Birtley but this ceased from 23rd May 1955 probably due to bus competition, the latter having a much more direct route. Note the remarkable array of signals of various vintages and pigeon lofts in adjacent properties. One wonders if any of the resident birds ever returned home when given their freedom bearing in mind this must have been one of the smokiest and noisiest locations in County Durham. *Rail Photoprints*

In about 1955 it was decided to modify a batch of ten BR Standard Class 9F 2-10-0s with Westinghouse air pumps to operate the discharge doors of the dedicated wagons used on these trains and Nos.92060 to 92066 plus 92097 to 92099 were allocated to Tyne Dock shed for use on the Consett workings. The Class 9Fs continued almost unchallenged until 19th November 1966 when the final steam workings took place prior to the introduction of diesel traction and local enthusiasts ensured the 9Fs would go out on a high note. The very last steam working was hauled by No.92063 which was in absolutely immaculate condition as a result of the efforts of the local BR staff ably assisted by enthusiastic photographers. Titled 'The Tyne Docker', the train left Tyne Dock at 10.00am and consisted of nine hopper wagons plus two brake vans, the first packed to the gunwales with enthusiasts. It is seen here at Pontop Crossing with the signal box and Newcastle to Sunderland line, which runs from left to right, behind the train. Following their takeover by diesel traction, these trains were diverted to run via Gateshead and the route from Boldon colliery to Washington was closed. *Terry Phillips*

A pair of Gresley-designed 2-6-2Ts, Nos.67647 and 67652, stand in Newcastle-upon-Tyne Central station some time in 1956; unfortunately no details of the train are available. While the locomotives appear to be identical they actually belong to two different classes: No.67652 is a V3 Class locomotive while No.67647 is one of the original V1 engines. The Class V1s were designed by Gresley, making their first appearance in 1930, and were originally intended for use on suburban services in the London area, but most spent their entire lives on similar duties in the Newcastle, Edinburgh and Glasgow areas. The LNER made a start on increasing the boiler pressure from 180lbs to 200lbs and the engines concerned were reclassified V3 although the two classes were indistinguishable externally. This policy was continued by BR and eventually a total of 73 locomotives was converted, including No.67647 which was modified in December 1959. *Rail Photoprints*

When the Class A4 Pacifics came to an end in September 1966 No.60019 *Bittern*, which had latterly been one of the star performers on the Glasgow to Aberdeen three-hour trains, was purchased privately for preservation. It was stored at York shed for a while following withdrawal but returned to the main line on 4th November 1967 when it was turned out to work an RCTS rail tour from Leeds to Edinburgh. *Bittern* is seen here taking water at Newcastle-upon-Tyne on the outward run and only a small group of enthusiasts visible on the platform suggest this was anything other than a normal scheduled passenger train. *Bittern* was a long-standing resident of Gateshead shed so it was very much on home territory. A few weeks before this tour ran a ban on steam had been announced by BR and the Scottish Region authorities had indicated that No.60019 would be the final steam locomotive they would accept, so there was a general feeling of gloom at Waverley station later in the day prior to *Bittern*'s departure. In the event the participants need not have worried! No.60019 put in a lively performance and regained time on every section, the late arrival in Leeds being by no means attributable to the locomotive. *Terry Phillips*

Weak winter sunshine brightens the scene as former North Eastern Railway Q6 Class 0-8-0 No.63368, hauling a train of 21-ton coal hopper wagons, takes the chord line at Boldon Colliery that enabled trains from the Gateshead direction to join the Washington to Tyne Dock route. The station, which is located on the Gateshead to Sunderland line, is on the extreme left of the picture that was taken on 19th November 1966. This was a typical 'day in, day out' job for these locomotives, menial in the extreme but absolutely vital for the local economy which, at that time, was based to a large degree on heavy industry. No.63368 had certainly earned its keep, being a Darlington product that entered service in August 1913; it was withdrawn just a few weeks after this picture was taken. *Terry Phillips*

The East Coast Main Line crosses the River Wansbeck just north of Morpeth on a high viaduct which takes the line over a deep ravine and in this shot J27 Class 0-6-0 No.65842, hauling a couple of brake vans, is seen riding high above the river which is out of sight, hidden by a dense covering of trees. These locomotives were one of the last pre-grouping classes to survive on BR in any number, a total of 115 being constructed at a variety of locations between 1906 and 1923. No.65842 was built by Beyer Peacock & Co. entering traffic in July 1908; it lasted until January 1967 when it was taken out of service. This photograph was taken on 19th March 1966. *John Boyes/ARPT*

When BR embarked on wholesale dieselisation it was obvious that, despite the huge number of locomotives being constructed by a variety of manufacturers, not every corner of their vast system could be modernised at once. It was decided that one of the last pockets of steam traction would be in the north-east and, as a result, the indigenous pre-grouping Class Q6 0-8-0s and J27 0-6-0s would have to remain in service until sufficient diesel replacements became available. Thus those locomotives became some of the longest serving engines on BR and Class J27 No.65811, seen here at Sunderland shed on 4th September 1967, was certainly one of those, being built by the North British Locomotive Co. and entering service in May 1908. Steam traction in the north-east came to an end five days later and with it No.65811's long career. *Rail Photoprints*

This picture gives a good idea of the very primitive conditions in which steam locomotives were maintained well into the 1960s. Here, five Class J27 0-6-0s accompanied by Class K1 2-6-0 No.62024 are congregated around the turntable at North Blyth shed where steam traction was used principally on coal trains to local power stations and suchlike. The age of technology was much acclaimed by politicians during that decade but none of it had apparently filtered down to North Blyth! There were two sheds at Blyth, South Blyth being on the south bank of the river Blyth whilst North Blyth shed was hidden away in dockland on the north bank, so train spotters had to take the ferry across the river if they wanted to visit both sheds. There was never a passenger service to North Blyth but South Blyth (the station was called simply 'Blyth') was served mainly by a shuttle service of trains from Newsham on the Newcastle-upon-Tyne to Newbiggin line; there was however a limited through service to and from Newcastle. Steam traction came to an end on the Blyth & Tyne section in June 1967 when diesels replaced the remaining steam locomotives. This picture was taken in October 1965. *Rail Photoprints*

The North British Railway had a modest network of branch lines in England which extended from Riccarton Junction, on the Edinburgh to Carlisle 'Waverley' route, through Reedsmouth to Hexham and Morpeth, and an associated short connection from Scotsgap to Rothbury. These routes served a remote and thinly populated area of Northumberland, the Reedsmouth to Morpeth and Scotsgap to Rothbury sections being very early closure casualties with passenger trains ceasing from 15th September 1952. Perhaps the most spectacular line in this area was the Hexham to Riccarton Junction line which traversed a wild and desolate landscape but survived until closure was effected on 15th October 1956. Despite the withdrawal of passenger services on the other routes goods workings continued, and there were even occasional passenger trains conveying troops to the various training camps in the area, but the end came on 4th October 1966 when the last remaining section, from Morpeth to Woodburn, was closed completely. The use of pre-grouping motive power was an additional bonus for railway photographers and in this shot former North Eastern Railway Class J27 No.65842, which had presumably benefited from 'unofficial' cleaning, is depicted climbing away from Woodburn on 22nd September 1966 with the weekly pick-up goods train just a few weeks before the final curtain came down on this little-known line. *John Boyes/ARPT*

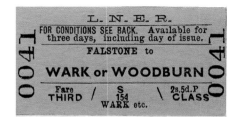

Playing to the gallery. Apart from BR's ludicrously expensive tour arranged for the following Sunday, the last day of standard gauge steam was 4th August 1968 and this proved to be a day of feverish activity throughout Lancashire as numerous societies had arranged tours to mark the sad, never-to-be-forgotten occasion. BR was probably hard-pressed to find sufficient locomotives in reasonable order and one or two engines were reportedly not up to the job as a result of faulty injectors or, in one case, a leaking tender. The Stephenson Locomotive Society ran two tours from Birmingham to cater for the unprecedented demand and here their 'Farewell to Steam No. 2' tour is seen making a very smoky assault in fine style on the climb to Copy Pit with 'Black Five' Nos. 44874 and 45017 in charge. *Author*